STERLING BIOGRAPHIES

Lewis & Clark

Blazing a Trail West

John Burrows

STERLING

New York / London
www.sterlingpublishing.com/kids

Without the near limitless patience, wise counsel, and experience of editors Susan Hoe and Kelly Smith this book would not be in your hands now. I am tremendously grateful for all their efforts. Much of the research for this book was done at the New York City Public Library main research branch. Its staff, collection, and technology system is a national treasure.

STERLING and the distinctive Sterling logo are registered trademarks of Sterling Publishing Co., Inc.

Library of Congress Cataloging-in-Publication Data

Burrows, John, 1972-
  Lewis and Clark : trailblazers / by John Burrows.
    p. cm. — (Sterling biographies)
  Includes index.
  ISBN-13: 978-1-4027-4533-1
  ISBN-10: 1-4027-4533-8
  1. Lewis, Meriwether, 1774-1809—Juvenile literature. 2. Clark, William, 1770-1838—Juvenile literature. 3. Explorers—West (U.S.)—Biography—Juvenile literature. 4. Lewis and Clark Expedition (1804-1806)—Juvenile literature. 5. West (U.S.)—Discovery and exploration—Juvenile literature. 6. West (U.S.)—Description and travel—Juvenile literature. I. Title.
  F592.7.L42B77 2008
  917.804′20922—dc22
  [B]
                                        2007050479

10 9 8 7 6 5 4 3 2 1

Published by Sterling Publishing Co., Inc.
387 Park Avenue South, New York, NY 10016
© 2008 by John Burrows
Distributed in Canada by Sterling Publishing
c/o Canadian Manda Group, 165 Dufferin Street
Toronto, Ontario, Canada M6K 3H6
Distributed in the United Kingdom by GMC Distribution Services
Castle Place, 166 High Street, Lewes, East Sussex, England BN7 1XU
Distributed in Australia by Capricorn Link (Australia) Pty. Ltd.
P.O. Box 704, Windsor, NSW 2756, Australia

Printed in China
All rights reserved

Sterling ISBN 978-1-4027-4533-1 (paperback)
         ISBN 978-1-4027-6059-4 (hardcover)

For information about custom editions, special sales, premium and corporate purchases, please contact Sterling Special Sales Department at 800-805-5489 or specialsales@sterlingpublishing.com.

Designed for SimonSays Design! by Frieda Christofides
Image research by Larry Schwartz

Contents

Events in the Life of Meriwether Lewis and William Clark

1770

August 1, 1770
William Clark is born in Caroline County, Virginia, to a plantation-owning family.

August 18, 1774
Meriwether Lewis is born in Charlottesville, Virginia, also to a plantation-owning family.

July 4, 1776–September 3, 1783
The American Revolutionary War is fought against the British.

October 1784–Spring 1785
William Clark's family moves to Kentucky.

1784
Lewis's family moves to Wilkes County, Georgia.

March 6, 1792
Clark becomes a lieutenant in the U.S. Army.

1795
Lewis joins the U.S. Army; meets Captain William Clark.

April 1, 1801
Lewis becomes the secretary to newly elected President Thomas Jefferson.

Summer–Fall 1802
Jefferson plans an expedition across the western territories with Lewis in command. Negotiations for the Louisiana Territory begin with France.

June 19, 1803
Lewis invites Clark to join the expedition which is to be called the Corps of Discovery.

July 4, 1803
France approves the Louisiana Purchase.

May–July 1803
Lewis attends science classes in Philadelphia and conducts initial preparations in Pittsburgh.

Winter 1803
Lewis and Clark set up camp where the Missouri and Mississippi Rivers meet; they spend the winter there preparing their men for the journey.

May 21, 1804,
The Corps of Discovery officially begins its journey, heading northwest on the Missouri River.

August 1804
The Corps of Discovery begins hosting council meetings with various local Indian tribes.

November 1804
The Corps meets the Mandan Indians and winters alongside them. There they meet Sacagawea.

April 7, 1805
The Corps continues westward. The keelboat is sent back to St. Louis with plant and animal samples.

June 13, 1805
Lewis reaches the Great Falls of the Missouri.

August 11, 1805
Lewis meets the Shoshone Indian Tribe. Sacagawea is reunited with her brother several days later.

September 9–October 7, 1805
The Corps treks through the Rocky Mountains, and then travels downriver by canoes they have made.

November 1805
The Corps reaches the mouth of the Columbia River. They build their winter quarters there.

March 20, 1806
The Corps starts its return journey back east.

July–August 1806
Lewis and Clark each take extended side trips. Lewis has a run-in with Blackfeet Indians. Clark explores parts of the Yellowstone River.

September 23, 1806
The Corps of Discovery reaches St. Louis. Lewis and Clark become instant celebrities.

March 1807
Lewis and Clark both receive various political and military appointments in the Louisiana Territory.

January 5, 1808
William Clark marries Julia Hancock.

October 11, 1809
Suffering from depression and alcoholism, Lewis takes his own life at an inn in Tennessee.

June 16, 1813
Clark is appointed Governor of the northern Louisiana Territory, later called the Missouri Territory.

Autumn 1820
Clark loses his bid for the governor of the new state of Missouri; retains duties as superintendent of Indian affairs.

September 1, 1838
William Clark dies after a brief illness.

1838

A Journey Bound by Friendship

Oh [Ocean] in view! O! the joy!
—William Clark

In November 1805, the expedition across North America led by William Clark and Meriwether Lewis first spotted the Pacific Ocean. The salt air filled their noses, and they heard the screeching of seabirds. Clark summed up his feelings in his journal, "Oh [Ocean] in view! O! the joy!"

Over the previous year and a half, they struggled against the currents of the Missouri River and risked death by grizzly bears and unfriendly Indian (**Native American**) tribes. They had survived scorching summers, and spent a freezing winter a thousand miles from any white-man's civilization. Near-starvation drove them to eat dogs and horses.

They persisted, and in the end, discovered dozens of rivers, two mountain ranges, and hundreds of plants and animals. Amazingly, only one man among the expedition died.

By reaching the Pacific, the **Corps** of Discovery had completed half of its mission—to explore the vast Louisiana Territory. They still had to get home but at least they knew the trip could be done. The strong friendship Lewis and Clark had forged throughout their journey had carried them across the continent. Together they knew they would get back alive.

CHAPTER 1

Similar Family Backgrounds

No season or circumstance could obstruct his purpose, plunging thro' the winter's snows and frozen streams in pursuit of his object.

—Thomas Jefferson, describing Lewis as a young boy

As children, Meriwether Lewis and William Clark shared similar family backgrounds. They were born within miles of one another in Virginia but never met as children. In order to acquire better farmland, both families eventually moved West—Lewis to Georgia and Clark to Kentucky.

The childhoods of Meriwether and William unfolded with parallel adventures as the young boys grew up on the frontier, learning many of the skills that were necessary for survival. Perhaps their similar backgrounds are what ultimately drew them together and gave them the courage and capacity to undertake one of the greatest expeditions in American history.

The Boyhood of Meriwether Lewis

On August 18, 1774, Lucy Meriwether Lewis gave birth to her first son, Meriwether, in Charlottesville, Virginia. She and her husband, William, already had one daughter named Jane. Another son, Reuben, would be born in 1777. Both Lucy and William came from prominent colonial families. Along with material wealth, the family enjoyed a high social standing.

A recent photograph shows Monticello, the home of Thomas Jefferson. It was built near Lewis's childhood home in Charlottesville, Virginia. Jefferson designed the mansion, which was completed in 1809.

On a distant hill from the Lewis home a grander house was being constructed. It was called Monticello and belonged to Thomas Jefferson, their neighbor and one of their closest friends. This neighbor would one day become president of the United States and would figure prominently in the later life of Meriwether Lewis.

In 1776, war broke out between **the thirteen colonies** and the British Empire. William Lewis enlisted in the newly formed **Continental army** as a lieutenant, but three years later died from pneumonia after falling into a river on a cold November day. Meriwether Lewis was just five years old.

Six months later, on May 13, 1780, his mother remarried—this time to John Marks, a captain in the Continental army. As the war wound down, Captain Marks began developing new plans for the family.

Virginia was getting crowded. The town of Charlottesville stood at the western edge of the settled British colonies. Beyond it lay wilderness, Indians, danger, and more land to farm. The Lewis farm grew tobacco, which was the most profitable American crop in the late 1700s. If a man wanted to get rich, growing tobacco was one way to do it. Marks decided he would acquire a bigger farm. Like thousands of other colonists, he looked westward for fresh planting grounds.

Thomas Jefferson (1743–1826)

At the time of Meriwether Lewis's birth, Thomas Jefferson was a plantation owner and a lawmaker in the Virginia colonial government. In the coming years, he became world famous as the father of modern democracy and the author of the Declaration of Independence. In 1801, he became the third president of the United States. Throughout his rise to fame and power, he remained close with Meriwether Lewis's family.

Jefferson's interests ranged from architecture to philosophy to science. He played the violin and spoke several languages. In addition, he practiced law and ran his plantation. When the United States broke away from England, he devoted his talents to the business of government. He served in the **legislature** of Virginia, as governor of Virginia, as a **minister** to France, and as the first **secretary of state** under President George Washington.

The third president of the United States, Thomas Jefferson was also an accomplished architect, statesman, and musician.

Life on the Frontier

Meriwether Lewis was eight years old when his family packed up and moved to Georgia. Once they settled in Wilkes County, Georgia, Meriwether worked alongside his parents. He learned how to hunt and to farm—skills that were essential for survival at the time.

One day, Meriwether and some friends went deer hunting. Meriwether's rifle was heavy and nearly as long as he was tall. It shot only one bullet at a time before needing to be reloaded—a time-consuming exercise. Thus, Meriwether kept his rifle loaded as he walked, in case he saw a deer to shoot.

As the group of friends crossed a field on the way back to the house, a bull that was on the loose spotted the boys. The bull—being a very territorial animal—charged at the boys, running at

Colonial farmers, like Lewis's father, used a type of plow shown in this modern photo to prepare the fields for planting.

Tobacco Farming in Early America

More than any other factor, tobacco pushed farmers westward in the early days of the United States. First introduced to the earliest European explorers by Native Americans, tobacco was a perfect product for the young country. It did not grow in Europe in the 1700s, but Europeans craved it. Unlike food crops grown in the United States, it did not spoil on the long sea journey. American planters could ship their tobacco across the ocean for a great profit.

However, that profit came at a cost. Tobacco took a toll on the soil by drawing all the nutrients from the ground and leaving the dirt unfit for future crops. In the 1700s, farmers had not yet learned much about using fertilizers to replenish the soil. This meant that tobacco planters had to constantly find new land to plant—which meant moving farther west.

This undated illustration shows a typical tobacco farm from the late 1700s. Tobacco was quite profitable, but it damaged the soil for future crops.

full speed with its sharp horns pointed forward. The other boys sprinted for safety. Lewis knew that in an open field, with no trees to climb or fences to duck through, the bull would catch them. Meriwether decided to stand his ground. With the bull charging toward him, he raised his rifle. He only had one shot, and he did not want to miss, so Meriwether waited until the bull was close enough. As the bull thundered toward him, he squeezed the trigger, calmly, as he had been taught. The shot struck home! The beast collapsed to the ground, a few feet before the young marksman. He had saved himself and his friends from the angry bull.

In later years, Meriwether Lewis would often show his sense of calm and bravery in the face of terrible danger as he traveled across the wildest part of North America.

The Boyhood of William Clark

William Clark was also born in Virginia. Four years older than Meriwether Lewis, William was born on August 1, 1770, to a big family headed by John and Ann Clark. He had five older brothers (Jonathan, George, John, Richard, and Edmund) and three older sisters (Ann, Lucy, and Eliza). Three years after William's birth, his little sister Frances was born, rounding out the number of Clark children to an even ten. Like Lewis's family, Clark's also owned a large tobacco plantation. During the **Revolutionary War** against Britain, the older Clark boys assumed high military ranks in the Continental army.

Older brother George rose to the rank of general and became a war hero—with some regarding him as highly as General George Washington. Eighteen years older than William, George Rogers Clark would be a father figure to his young brother.

Fighting the British and the Indians

When most people think of the Revolutionary War, they usually remember the clashes fought against the British—such as the Battles of Lexington and Concord and the Battle of Bunker Hill, all in Massachusetts.

While George Washington led armies on the East Coast—in Pennsylvania, New York, and New Jersey—George Rogers Clark fought in the Ohio River Valley, which ranged as far west as St. Louis—the city that would be the official starting point of his younger brother William's famous expedition across the continent years later.

Instead of fighting British soldiers, George Clark's men mainly battled Indians, who fought in a manner that would now be called guerilla warfare. This meant they would fight at night and would stage **ambushes**. Even though the Indians were allied with the British, they were also fighting for their own land and for their very survival—which meant they fought with great passion. The Americans were struggling for their survival as well, so when Indian and American forces met in battle, the clash was brutal on both sides.

George Rogers Clark, the eldest brother of William Clark, was a great general of the Revolutionary War. This portrait shows him at the height of his career.

Like the Lewis family, the Clark family decided to move westward at the end of the war in 1783 in order to obtain larger tracts of land for their plantation. Almost ten years before, George Clark had begun acquiring land in Kentucky, along Beargrass Creek near Louisville. When the war ended, William's older brother Jonathan headed for Kentucky with one of their young slaves named York, who would help him clear the land. The rest of the family would follow a year later.

Traveling by Water

When the Clarks were ready to make their move, they traveled northwest through the inland hills and forests to the Monongahela River, near Pittsburgh, Pennsylvania. They hired a boat to take them south on the Monongahela and onto the Ohio River where they floated south to Louisville. There were a number of reasons the Clarks took such a roundabout route.

The roads in the late 1700s were very poor for travel even over short distances, and as one traveled farther west and south, they were even worse. The Clarks were traveling with all their worldly possessions. Traveling through that territory with heavy, overloaded wagons would have been extremely difficult, if not impossible.

Indians also posed another danger to settlers who were moving into the western edge of the colonies. These Native Americans saw the white newcomers as a threat to their land and fought aggressively to protect it. A large family like the Clarks, burdened with silver teapots and slaves, furniture, plows, and cattle, would have been vulnerable to Indian attack if they chose to travel by wagons that simply lumbered down narrow rutted paths.

The Clarks left Virginia in October of 1784, when William was fourteen years old. They reached Redstone, Pennsylvania—the first leg of their journey—where they arranged for the

The Slave York

The early American economy depended on slavery. The primary cash crop, tobacco, required heavy labor for planting, harvesting, **curing** the leaves, and shipping. Slaves did the work. Captured in West Africa, they were packed onto ships and brought to America for sale. Many died during the journey; more suffered horribly at the hands of their slave owners.

But the relationship between slaves and their owners was often complicated, and no one demonstrated this fact more clearly than York, whose parents were owned by the Clark family. When York was born in 1770—the same year of William Clark's birth—he too became the property of the Clark family. However, he also became young William's first best friend and playmate.

As they grew older, the lives of York and William remained intertwined. Just as York accompanied Jonathan to Kentucky to help clear the land, he would also accompany William Clark on the momentous journey to the Pacific.

York, as seen in this painting, was William Clark's companion from childhood through most of his adult life. He accompanied the Clark family to Kentucky and later helped Clark explore the Louisiana Territory.

The Clark family traveled down the Monongahela River on a flatboat similar to the one in this image from the mid-1800s. Broad and cumbersome, flatboats were built to carry lots of cargo, including livestock.

purchase of a flatboat—a broad, cumbersome boat like a barge that could hold all their belongings. They were ready to continue their trip on water, when an early winter froze the Monongahela River, locking the flatboat in ice. Unable to travel, the family spent the winter in Redstone.

In late February 1785, the ice on the Monongahela finally melted. The family loaded their flatboat and began their journey down the river. While the river was safer than the roads, it still held many perils.

They had been warned about Indian tribes along the river. Their friends told them to travel at night and to try to keep moving. If they did stop along the way for any length of time, local tribes could learn of their presence and attack them. So for much of the journey down the river, the Clark family glided silently through the night. The wild country unfurled in the darkness alongside their crowded boat, which was packed with all their possessions and livestock.

This image from 1873 depicts a conflict that played out across North America. While Native Americans fought to keep white settlers off their land, the newcomers fought to establish new homesteads.

The importance of their friends' advice became even clearer when they stopped to visit at the cabin of Robert and Mary Elliott on March 3. The Clarks were probably expecting that the Elliotts would invite them to have dinner and spend the night in their cabin. However, no invitation was offered, so the Clarks sailed a bit farther down river and set up a camp for the night.

That night a party of Indians attacked the Elliott cabin. They killed and scalped all the men. Only Mary and her daughter escaped alive. The Clark family was now intimately aware of the dangerous nature of this new territory as they continued on to Louisville.

Life in Kentucky

William Clark was fifteen years old when they reached Louisville. The family unloaded their boat at Beargrass Creek, where they built a long frame house near a great waterfall. They called their new estate Mulberry Hill.

Clark quickly adapted to frontier life. He became an expert shot with a rifle. Among his favorite pastimes was a sport called "barking squirrels." To play the game, William and his friends looked for a squirrel that was perched on a branch. When one was spotted, one of the boys would raise his rifle and shoot—not at the squirrel, but at the slender limb on which the rodent sat. Once the branch was struck, the unharmed squirrel would be flicked into the air.

Hitting the narrow tree bough required a high level of marksmanship and this sport provided good survival training in case of Indian attacks—even for boys as young as William.

Mulberry Hill, the frontier home of the Clark family, fell into disrepair by the late 1800s, as shown in this picture from the time. It was completely demolished in 1912.

CHAPTER 2

Army Life

*I am situated on the Monongahela, about fifteen
miles above Pittsburgh where we shall be forted in
the winter. . . . I am quite delighted with the
soldier's life.*
        —Meriwether Lewis, 1794

Over the years, Indian attacks in the Kentucky Territory
had become frequent. A call went out for young men to
join the local militia to fight against them. The militia was
a type of volunteer fighting unit that was common in the
late 1700s. It was usually created for a specific local
purpose—like fighting Indians or fighting the British.
Standing more than six feet tall, William Clark had the
makings of a good militiaman: He was a strong horseman
and an excellent marksman, and although he had no
formal education to speak of, he did have a sharp mind
and was a natural leader.

At the age of 19, Clark joined
the Kentucky Militia. An
undated photograph shows
men wearing original uniforms
of the same militia and
standing before a blockhouse,
a type of fort commonly built
on the frontier.

In 1789, nineteen-year-old William Clark signed up for the Kentucky Militia, and over the next three years, he traveled back and forth between his home at Mulberry Hill and his militia unit. This unit had begun as a group of about two hundred men, but had grown to more than eight hundred. Despite Clark's skill and the increased size of his militia, peace with the Indians seemed distant. Settlers clamored for the U.S. Army to send additional help.

The Whiskey Rebellion

At the same time, there was trouble mounting with the farmers in western Pennsylvania and in the Kentucky and Ohio territories over a federal whiskey tax that they saw as unfair. In 1794, many settlers in Kentucky refused to pay the tax and threatened to secede from the United States, to start their own country. President George Washington feared that the newly formed America would crumble if this insurgency known as the Whiskey Rebellion continued. He took fast action on both fronts. First, he sent regular army troops to the region to help fight the Indians. Next, he called for the creation of a militia to fight the rebellious settlers in the Kentucky territories.

This illustration from 1794 shows a mob in western Pennsylvania tarring and feathering a tax inspector at the beginning of the Whiskey Rebellion.

Making Whiskey

Whiskey was a valuable commodity in the late 1700s. It was made from corn, and many of the farmers who lived in the western reaches of the United States grew corn among their crops. To make whiskey from corn, a large quantity of corn was mixed with water and yeast, and then allowed to ferment. This was called a mash, and once it had fermented, it was distilled— a process that used heat to extract the alcohol from the mash. The alcohol produced was whiskey.

For corn farmers, whiskey provided added economic benefits: The whiskey produced from the large quantities of corn was worth more money than the corn used to make it. In addition, whiskey was easier to ship to market for sale.

An 1867 wood engraving depicts whiskey distillers hiding their stills deep in the woods and working at night to avoid detection.

William Clark, having already distinguished himself as a militiaman, was nominated for a commission as a lieutenant in the regular army on March 6, 1792.

Thirteen thousand young men volunteered to fight against the Whiskey Rebellion. Eighteen-year-old Meriwether Lewis was one of them. Like many of the other young soldiers, he signed up for the militia in a quest for adventure. He was raised on stories of the American Revolution, and on tales of military glory. This was his chance to grab a little glory for himself.

Lewis took the lowest rank in the militia when he volunteered as a private. For most soldiers this meant hardship. Meriwether, however, liked trekking across new territory with his fellow soldiers, looking for a fight. He built friendships with the officers. Those friendships, in turn, helped him advance quickly through the ranks. By the autumn of 1794, he had been promoted to the rank of ensign. He was now an officer.

In December of 1794, Lewis wrote to his mother, "I am situated on the Monongahela, about fifteen miles above Pittsburgh where we shall be forted in the winter....I am quite delighted with the soldier's life."

Lewis Joins the U.S. Army

The Whiskey Rebellion collapsed without a real fight. No longer needed, the militia was disbanded. In 1795, while most of the other men went back to their homes, Lewis enlisted in the U.S. Army. The reason he gave for staying on in the military foretold of his future as an explorer. He wrote to his mother that no other occupation could satisfy his "passion for rambling."

As much as Lewis loved military life, he had two other passions that quickly caused trouble for him: alcohol and politics. Both would plague him later in life. Many young officers drank socially. Meriwether Lewis was not special in this regard. However, he may have drank more than other soldiers and his personality may have changed for the worse when intoxicated. It is known that he often started arguments with fellow soldiers— usually about politics—when he drank.

On the night of September 24, 1795, Meriwether Lewis stormed in on a group of other officers who had gathered to play cards. He was drunk, and he wanted to talk about politics. The other officers did not, so they asked him to leave. When he did not leave, they kicked him out. A short while later, a hostile Lewis returned and challenged one of the officers, Lieutenant Eliott, to a duel.

Duels

In the late 1700s, duels were illegal but common in the army. When one man had a dispute with another, he challenged his opponent to a duel. To refuse the challenge was considered dishonorable. After setting terms and weapons, usually pistols, they would go to a field with their weapons. Standing apart from one another at a set distance, they took aim and fired. The winner was whichever man remained standing after the shots were fired. Duels solved nothing. One man died or was horribly wounded and, usually, the other lived. Sometimes both men shot well and both men died.

Duels were once common and accepted. This image shows Vice President Aaron Burr preparing to duel former Secretary of the Treasury Alexander Hamilton in 1804. Hamilton died as a result.

General Anthony Wayne was the commanding officer of both Lewis and Clark. He assigned Lewis to Clark's unit in 1795, thereby starting the historic friendship.

Despite army regulations against duels, several generals disliked the other option almost as much. Men with genuine disputes were supposed to file for a court martial, or trial, to resolve major differences. Court martials presented a lot of trouble for generals, so many of them turned a blind eye to the duels among their officers. General Anthony Wayne, Lewis's commanding officer, was this kind of general.

Lieutenant Eliott knew that duels were illegal. Rather than accept Lewis's challenge, Eliott filed charges with General Wayne against Lewis. Although General Wayne did not want to hold a trial, he did convene a jury in his quarters on November 6, 1795. Eliott read his charges, claiming that before Meriwether Lewis had challenged him to a duel, Lewis had "Abruptly and in an Ungentleman like manner, when intoxicated, enter[ed] his house on 24the of September last, and without provocation, insult[ed] him and disturb[ed] the peace and harmony of a Company of Officers whom he had invited there." Lewis entered a plea of "not guilty." The trial lasted a week. When the jury declared Lewis "not guilty," General Wayne wrote that he "fondly hopes, as this is the first, that it also may be the last instance in [this command] of convening a court for a trial of this nature." To avoid any more disputes between the two men, General Wayne decided that Lewis needed to be transferred.

Lewis and Clark Meet

William Clark had accepted a commission as a lieutenant in the regular army in 1792. Over the next three years, he rose steadily through the ranks, impressing all the other officers above him with his competence and calm under fire and during negotiations with Indian tribes. Perhaps General Wayne thought that these traits suited him well to leading the hot-headed Meriwether Lewis. Thus, Meriwether Lewis was transferred to the Chosen Rifle Company commanded by Captain William Clark.

Perhaps General Wayne thought that these traits suited him well to leading the hot-headed Meriwether Lewis.

Six months after Lewis joined his unit, William Clark resigned from the army. He was twenty-five years old. He planned to go home to Mulberry Hill and build a life as a civilian. Brief though it may have been, the influence of William Clark seemed to have done Meriwether Lewis a world of good. In the months after he joined Clark's unit, he straightened up and rose in rank. On March 3, 1799, Lewis achieved the rank of lieutenant.

Soon Lewis was appointed as the regimental paymaster for the army. It was an important job that sent him all over the country. He often went into the frontier, dispersing money to the most distant army units scattered in the wilderness. The travel appealed to Lewis, and his avowed love of "rambling." More importantly, it allowed Lewis to meet other officers in the army. He learned their politics and their loyalties. This knowledge proved invaluable as he faced his next challenge.

CHAPTER 3

In the Service of Thomas Jefferson

Of courage undaunted . . . I could have no hesitation in confiding the enterprise to [Meriwether Lewis].

—Thomas Jefferson

In 1800, Meriwether Lewis's old neighbor and family friend Thomas Jefferson became the third president of the United States, beating out the incumbent President John Adams. He now needed an assistant, or secretary, and he knew exactly who to hire for the job. Eleven days before taking office, on February 23, 1801, Jefferson wrote to Meriwether Lewis and offered the job to him. The president told Lewis that as the secretary to the president, Lewis would meet many important people. Lewis accepted the job immediately and officially became Jefferson's secretary on April 1, 1801.

Jefferson's wife had died many years earlier, and he never remarried. His children were fully grown and lived with their

Meriwether Lewis, seen here in a c. 1807 portrait by Charles Willson Peale, entered into the service of Thomas Jefferson just a few years earlier.

families. So for most of the time Jefferson and Lewis stayed in the vast White House alone. When they ate dinner together, Jefferson, one of America's most brilliant minds, tutored Lewis on subjects ranging from politics to botany. On many evenings, visiting diplomats, politicians, and foreign leaders ate with them. Lewis took in all the wisdom that surrounded him.

Jefferson Looks Westward

When Thomas Jefferson took office, the United States was limited in size. The Atlantic Ocean bound it in the east, the Mississippi River in the west. To the north lay Canada, a territory controlled by the British Empire. Spain held what is now Florida. The funnel-shaped area that ran west of the Mississippi along the Missouri River and to the Rocky Mountains was owned by France. This swath of land—the Louisiana Territory—was vast and almost completely unexplored.

This map shows the United States as it stood in 1803. The Louisiana Territory is at the center of the map. The territory covered as much land as the 16 states of the time.

Early Attempts to Explore the West

At the end of the Revolutionary War, Jefferson wanted to raise money for an exploration of the West—all the land from the Mississippi to the Pacific—even though the United States controlled none of it. The money, however, could not be raised, and the plan was shelved. Exploration attempts of the West followed in the coming years. All failed, mostly because the explorers themselves underestimated the difficulty of the task.

In 1786, a man named John Ledyard approached Jefferson, then minister to France, with a plan to explore North America by traveling overland through Europe and Russia then crossing the Pacific Ocean to North America. He would continue eastward until he reached Washington, D.C. Ledyard made it only as far as Siberia.

In 1790, an army lieutenant named John Armstrong was sent to explore the Louisiana Territory. He brought no special equipment for navigation or wilderness survival. When Armstrong reached the Mississippi, he quit. He wrote of the expedition, "This is a business much easier planned than executed."

Two years later, in 1792, Jefferson again wanted to fund a mission to explore the west overland. Although eighteen-year-old Meriwether Lewis volunteered to lead the expedition, Jefferson knew the boy was too young

John Ledyard planned to explore North America by going around the world and starting from the Pacific Coast.

to lead the journey. Instead, he sent French **botanist** André Michaux, who got no farther than Kentucky.

The West remained unexplored, and Jefferson pushed it to the back of his mind until he became president.

What lay beyond the Mississippi River? The question gnawed at Jefferson for almost his entire life. Those millions of acres could contain unimaginable wonders. Jefferson wondered if wooly mammoths—giant, fur-covered, elephant-like prehistoric beasts—thundered across the unexplored prairie and were perhaps stalked by lost tribes of ancient Europeans who had crossed into North America long before Columbus arrived. How many undiscovered plants grew in the Louisiana Territory? Unknown fruits and grains, as well as entirely new types of foods might sprout from the earth.

This swath of land—the Louisiana Territory—was vast and almost completely unexplored.

In addition to his questions about the animals and plants that grew in the unknown territory, Jefferson had one other nagging question about the West—one that dated back to the time of Columbus. Was there an easy water route across the continent to the Pacific Ocean? If such a route—called the Northwest Passage—were found, it would change the world. An easy passage through the Louisiana Territory would mean goods from the United States could be shipped directly across the country to the Pacific Ocean. They could then be loaded onto oceangoing ships bound for China and India. In return, goods from Asia could be shipped straight across the Pacific for American ports in the Northwest.

Jefferson's limitless curiosity about science, plants, animals, geography, and anthropology—the study of human cultural and social behavior—was reinforced by a desire to help America prosper. Even before he became president and almost before the smoke had cleared after the American Revolution, Jefferson had begun thinking about an expedition to explore the vast territory.

The Louisiana Purchase

In 1801, President Jefferson received the printed account of a Scotsman named Alexander Mackenzie, who, in 1793, had traveled across Canada and had reached the western shore of Vancouver. This news alarmed Jefferson, and he sprang into action.

Mackenzie was a British subject. His trek across Canada maintained Britain's claim to land stretching from the Atlantic Ocean all the way across the continent to the Pacific. If the British secured trading routes and roads to Vancouver, British influence would creep southward, blocking the United States from the Pacific forever.

When Scottish-Canadian explorer Alexander Mackenzie reached the Pacific Ocean, he marked this rock near Vancouver. Word of his trip prompted the exploration of the Louisiana Territory.

The American exploration of the West had to begin immediately. This time Jefferson had the full strength of the office of president behind him. As commander-in-chief of the armed forces, he would send a military unit to conduct the explorations. However, the United States had no rights to any land between the Pacific and the Mississippi, which was owned by France.

Fortunately for Jefferson, in August 1802, France was having its own set of problems. A revolt in Haiti had undermined its holdings in the **New World**. Napoleon Bonaparte, the leader of France, knew that the Americans wanted to move into the Louisiana Territory. The only way he could protect the land

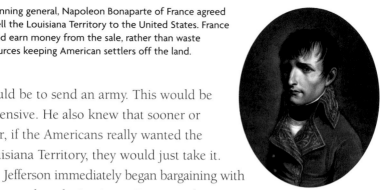

A cunning general, Napoleon Bonaparte of France agreed to sell the Louisiana Territory to the United States. France would earn money from the sale, rather than waste resources keeping American settlers off the land.

would be to send an army. This would be expensive. He also knew that sooner or later, if the Americans really wanted the Louisiana Territory, they would just take it.

Jefferson immediately began bargaining with France to buy the Louisiana Territory. There was no promise that France would let the land go. However, both Jefferson and Lewis had high hopes. They assumed that France would *not* transfer control of the Louisiana Territory before the U.S. expedition was set to begin. In order to avoid ruining the deal, Jefferson very carefully listed instructions that showed the expedition was to be a scientific as well as a mapmaking journey. A scientific expedition rather than one of expansion was less likely to upset the French. The expedition was called the Corps of Discovery, to underscore its scientific goals.

On July 4, 1803, word arrived from France that it would sell the Louisiana Territory to the United States for the sum of $15,000,000. It was a great birthday present for the fledgling United States. The formal transfer of power between France and the United States would

The Louisiana Purchase Treaty, shown here, was a monumental transaction both for America and for France. It doubled the size of the fledgling United States and freed France to focus on its other territories.

come the following year, just before the Corps of Discovery was scheduled to set out on this epic journey.

Lewis Selected as Expedition Leader

Lewis and Jefferson carefully read MacKenzie's account of his Canadian journey. It proved without a doubt that an explorer could cross the continent. Who would lead the U.S. expedition acrossto the Pacific? Lewis volunteered, and Jefferson accepted his offer.

Not everyone agreed with Jefferson's choice. Some thought that the job called for an experienced naturalist—a scientist. Lewis had not even attended college. However, Jefferson knew that while Lewis was not a scientist, Lewis had a sharp mind and was an able woodsman. It would be easier to train Lewis as a scientist than to train a scientist as a military leader and woodsman.

To further Lewis's education, Jefferson sent him for special training in Philadelphia with the best scientific minds that the United States had to offer. While studying there, Lewis could also begin making purchases for the expedition.

Lewis volunteered, and Jefferson accepted his offer.

Lewis decided he needed nineteen servicemen: fifteen privates and three sergeants, plus a corporal. All had to be of the highest caliber. The men could be recruited along the way to the expedition's true starting place in St. Louis. At the beginning, though, he needed to find a wise, experienced officer who was also a woodsman with mapmaking skills. His first choice was his old friend William Clark.

Lewis wrote a letter to Clark on June 19, 1803, explaining his strategy for the expedition. "My plan: it is to descend the Ohio in a

This c. 1810 portrait by Charles Willson Peale shows William Clark as the statesman and politician he would become after returning from the journey to explore the Louisiana Territory.

keeled boat, then to prepare to . . . pass over the waters of the Columbia or Oregon and by that means reach the western ocean."

Clark replied immediately, "The enterprise is much as I have long anticipated and am much pleased with—and as my situation in life will admit the absence by the length of time necessary to accompany you on undertaking I will cheerfully join you."

Equal in Every Way

When Lewis asked William Clark to join the expedition, he offered him the chance to return to the army at the rank he had left—that of captain. Clark might have refused the job if he had been offered a lesser rank. Unfortunately, the military officials did not know of Lewis's offer, and they processed Clark's rank and pay as that of a lieutenant. In the official eyes of the army, Lewis was the sole leader of the expedition. Clark was his junior officer.

The mistake embarrassed Lewis and angered Clark. To save face, Lewis proposed a solution. The two men, he said, would share command and leadership roles. They would not tell the men in the Corps of Discovery that Clark's official rank was lower than Lewis's. If the men under their command believed that Clark was a captain, then it was just as good. Clark thought this an imperfect solution, but he had no better plan. He agreed with Lewis. For the rest of the journey, Lewis referred to Clark as a captain, who was "equal in all respects." None of the men under them ever knew differently.

Preparing for the Expedition

The Object of your mission is to explore the Missouri river, & such principal stream of it, as . . . may offer the most direct & practicable water communication across this continent, for the purpose of commerce.

—Thomas Jefferson

In agreement with Jefferson's plan, Lewis went to Philadelphia for classes in botany and astronomy. Despite his lack of formal education, Lewis had a strong foundation of general knowledge and a hungry mind. As a boy, he had taught himself the constellations of the night sky—a skill necessary for any celestial navigation.

Having spent so much time in the wilderness, he had an excellent eye for distinguishing differences in the plant world. He studied examples of plants known to man so that he could recognize them when he saw them. No doubt, he would also find plants that were unknown to science, so he learned the proper method of naming plants and animals in Latin.

There would be no doctor on the expedition. As the officers in charge, Lewis and Clark would be responsible for the medical needs of their men. With this in mind, Lewis studied with Dr. Benjamin Rush, one of the most

Dr. Benjamin Rush (1745–1813)

Dr. Benjamin Rush was not just a doctor. He was also a statesman and a signer of the Declaration of Independence, as well as a businessman. He had been the **surgeon general** to the Continental army during the Revolutionary War and established the first free medical clinic in the United States.

Despite these great achievements, Dr. Rush is now best recalled for one of the medicines he gave to Lewis for the journey. Dr. Rush claimed these dense balls of medicine effectively treated most of the illnesses that the men would face. A compound of mercury, chlorine, and an extract from morning glory plants, Rush's pills were called "thunderclappers" because they provoked a hurried trip to the toilet with explosive results. For some diseases, they were perfect. They helped the patient expel toxins from his system rapidly so that the body could begin to heal. For patients already suffering from diarrhea and dehydration, Dr. Rush's pills might have been among the worst things anyone could administer.

Dr. Benjamin Rush, shown in this 1802 engraving, was a physician, politician, and business man.

well-known physicians of his days. However, given the low-level medical knowledge of the times, much of Rush's advice seemed more commonsensical than medical. For instance, he told Lewis that after very hard work, it would be more restful for his men to lay down, rather than sit:

A Long Shopping List

All of the earlier expeditions to the West failed partly because they were poorly outfitted with navigational and camping equipment. If those expeditions had gone any farther, they might also have failed because they were poorly armed. When Lewis started planning the trip, he compiled a long list of materials that he would need. He expected to be away for a long time without access to any stores, so his list covered everything from mapmaking tools—an assortment of compasses, a **sextant**, pens, paper, and a chronometer (clock)—to camping gear, tents, knives, pots, pans, and hatchets.

Although Lewis's original budget was $2,500—a huge sum of money at the time—and the items he purchased were considered very expensive, he allotted the largest portion of his budget, $696, to "Indian presents." Because President Jefferson had mandated that the Corps of Discovery befriend any of the tribes that they met along the way, Lewis carried a large stock of gifts for the Indians including a bunch of useful items—such as knives, fishing hooks, pocket telescopes, thimbles, and kettles—as well as trinkets such as ribbon, glass beads, and earrings.

Lewis's original shopping list for supplies included presents for the Indians he would meet while exploring the West.

In addition to all the equipment and Indian presents, Lewis also purchased weapons to take on the journey. He chose what he called the Pennsylvania short rifle. These were muzzle-loading rifles with a three-foot-long barrel. In order to shoot one, a rifleman poured a few grains of gunpowder down the muzzle of the weapon.

Blunderbusses, like this one shown, were short, powerful guns. The Corps of Discovery mounted them on swivels on the keelboat.

He then rammed down a bit of packing material, followed by a lead ball that was a half-inch in diameter. After pulling the trigger and shooting the gun, the whole process was repeated.

New Boat Designs

Lewis designed two boats especially for the trip. The first one was a flat-bottomed boat with a keel and rigging for sails. Although these keelboats had been used on the rivers of America since its founding, Lewis's design differed in its size. He wanted a large boat that could carry more men, more supplies, and more samples of what they found. This big boat would be the flagship of the trip.

A replica of the keelboat used by Lewis and Clark shows the sail riggings and a blunderbuss mounted on the aft cabin of the boat.

The second boat design was more novel and ambitious. It had an iron framework that could be disassembled and packed onto the flatboat, which would transport it up the Missouri River and into the mountains of the West. When the expedition reached the end of the Missouri, the men could carry this framework over land. When another river was reached, the men would assemble the framework and cover it with animal hides that were then sealed with tar. By using this original boat design, Lewis would have a large, light, and portable boat available throughout the journey. It would provide them with an easy passage to the Pacific Ocean. That was the plan at least.

Even though the iron-framed boat was a new idea, its construction went fairly smoothly. It was the flat-bottomed keelboat that caused the most problems.

Long Delays

In order to carry out his keelboat boat design, Lewis traveled to Pittsburgh and hired a boatbuilder, who was unfortunately an alcoholic. Because of his constant drinking, the boatbuilding went slowly. Lewis ordered the man to work faster, but it did no good. Sadly, there were no other boatbuilders available to complete the work. Lewis waited.

During the long wait, Lewis walked around and explored Pittsburgh. One day, he spotted a dog—a black Newfoundland—which he bought for himself. He named it Seaman and planned to take the dog on the expedition with him.

Seaman, the Newfoundland dog that Lewis bought while awaiting construction of the keelboat, traveled all the way to the Pacific and back again with the expedition.

Early on August 31, 1803, the boatbuilder finally finished his work. Lewis wasted no time. Three hours after the last plank of the boat had been laid, he had the boat packed with all of the supplies he had purchased in Philadelphia. Anything that did not fit would be either carried by cart over roads or loaded into pirogues, a type of flat-bottomed canoe. He was determined to get underway from Pittsburgh and start the first leg of the trip to St. Louis. But first, he planned to stop off in Kentucky to pick up William Clark.

Traveling Down the Ohio

Looking out on the Ohio River—he was packed and ready to go—Lewis could see rocks jutting above the water surface. Rivers rise and fall with the seasons. The level of a river falls during the summer. In a time of drought, a river's level can drop so much that a large boat cannot float downstream.

People warned Lewis. They had never seen the Ohio River so low. However, Lewis had no choice. If he did not make the journey now, the trip could be delayed by as much as a year, while he waited for rains to replenish the flow of the river. He decided to take the risk.

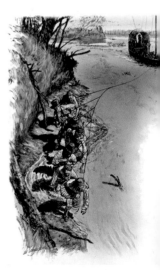

As he sailed down the Ohio, Lewis felt like the bottom of his boat struck every boulder and stump in the river. To lighten the load on the keelboat, he purchased another canoe to carry some excess weight. At times, the men he recruited had to get out of the boat and drag it over the shallows. It was very slow going.

Travel against the Missouri's current was hard work. When the river was too low, the men had to pull the keelboat up the river, as they are seen doing in this image.

A Reunion of Two Friends

Lewis finally arrived at William Clark's home on October 15, 1803. Officially, the expedition had not begun yet. That would happen in St. Louis. However, it must have been a wonderful moment for Lewis to tie off his boat and walk over to the cabin Clark shared with his brother George. It was a chance to talk to an old friend and a chance to rest his body, which was sore and tired from the difficult trip down the nearly dry Ohio River.

In Clarkesville, Kentucky, the size of the expedition expanded. Clark had already interviewed some local men as potential recruits for the Corps of Discovery. Now that Lewis was present, the two men could choose more. Of those who joined the expedition at this point, one stood out. George Drouillard—whose name Lewis and Clark never learned to spell properly—was of French and Indian descent. He had grown up as a woodsman, spending equal amounts of time living among white settlers and Native Americans. He spoke several Indian languages, including a form of sign language that was universal across several tribes. His skill with a rifle was legendary, as were his capabilities as a **tracker**. Lewis was glad to have him along.

Georges Drouillard was part French and part Indian. His skill as a translator, woodsman, and hunter made him indispensable to Lewis and Clark.

At this point, the size of the expedition included three sergeants and fifteen men, plus Lewis and Clark. Each sergeant would command a unit of five men called a "mess." Each mess was a self-contained unit responsible for all its own daily chores like cooking, cleaning, and setting up camp. When they left Kentucky, Lewis decided that he had enough men.

Stopping for Winter

It was late November 1803, when the Corps of Discovery floated down the Ohio and into the Mississippi River. From Pittsburgh to this point, the expedition had already covered nearly one thousand miles.

They traveled north, making their way to the mouth of the Missouri River. The Missouri would be the route for most of the journey. The power of this river surprised Lewis. The mud-laden waters churned against the boats as the men struggled to row and paddle against the current. Lewis

The Missouri would be the route for most of the journey.

realized that he did not have enough men to contend with the river's powerful force. He decided he would recruit another fifteen men for the expedition upon reaching St. Louis.

Winter was fast approaching, so the expedition set up quarters a few miles north of St. Louis, on the opposite side of the Mississippi, in what is now the state of Illinois. They called this Camp Dubois, or Camp Wood. The camp looked out onto the spot where the two great rivers—the Mississippi and the Missouri—came together.

With more men, they needed more rifles, tents, blankets, and food. Jefferson had given Lewis a letter of credit from the government. This letter was used like a credit card would be

The men of the Corps of Discovery spent the winter of 1803–1804 at Camp Dubois. They celebrated Christmas by shooting rifles into the air.

today. Whatever Lewis wanted to buy, whatever he needed, the bill would go to the U.S. federal government.

St. Louis was still under the control of the French, and it was a bustling frontier town. Once the local shopkeepers learned that Lewis had a letter of credit, and that he could afford to pay almost any price for the goods that he needed, they raised their prices. Lewis fumed at first, but there was little he could do about the situation. He wrote the **IOUs** to the shopkeepers, instructing them to send the bills to Washington, and they did. This free-spending habit would come back to haunt Lewis.

The day finally arrived in May of 1804, when all the preparations were done. They had purchased extra nails, lard, wood, barrels, and whiskey for the journey. They had sailcloth and a small cannon mounted at the front of the keelboat. Throughout the winter at Camp Dubois, Clark had trained the men and overseen improvements to the keelboat. The Corps of Discovery was ready for the official start of its journey of exploration.

CHAPTER 5

Getting Under Way

Set out at half-past three o'clock, under three cheers from the gentle-men on the bank.
—William Clark, May 21, 1804

On the day the Corps of Discovery was ready to depart, rain poured down and delayed the group's departure for one day. When the rain showed no signs of stopping—not even for this historic occasion—the team pushed off anyway on May 21, 1804, and turned upstream into the current of the Missouri River.

The plan was a simple one. The Corps of Discovery would travel upstream on the Missouri until it reached its end. After that, Lewis and Clark would be heading into uncharted territory. They knew that a large mountain range stood between their starting point in St. Louis and their ultimate destination—the Pacific Ocean. They would have to cross the mountains and search for the Columbia River—a waterway that was discovered in 1792 by a sea captain from Boston. This river would be the final path to the Pacific.

The Corps of Discovery would travel upstream on the Missouri until they reached its end.

The first part of the trip along the Missouri River—a waterway that was discovered by French explorers Louis Joliet and Jacques Marquette in 1673—covered fairly well-known territory. At night, they would anchor the keelboat and pull up the pirogues and make camp. President Jefferson had charged Lewis and Clark with exploring the entire territory drained by the Missouri River. This meant that they would frequently stop their travels and explore the surrounding area.

This c. 1911 print depicts French explorers Marquette and Joliet, the first Europeans to reach the Missouri River in 1673.

An Early Brush With Danger

Of all the dangers that lay before the men—hostile Indians, disease, bitter weather, and wild animals—the greatest one they faced was their own carelessness. Lewis, as commander of the expedition, demonstrated this on the second official day of the expedition.

Along parts of the Missouri, steep bluffs rose straight up from its banks. These bluffs were sandy hills with cliff-like sides along the river's edge. Having stopped to do some exploring, Lewis saw an especially towering bluff—about three hundred feet high. He decided to climb it. As he stood atop that bluff, he must have felt like he could see forever, over the rolling hills and on into the West. Lost in the natural beauty that surrounded him, Lewis stepped too close to the edge of the bluff. The edge collapsed under his weight, and he skidded down the steep slope

On the second day of the journey, Lewis nearly tumbled to his death, falling from a 300-foot-tall bluff. Fortunately, he caught himself after falling just 20 feet.

toward the churning river. After stumbling down twenty feet, he managed to stop his fall. Clark, writing about the incident in his journal remarked dryly, ". . . a fair evening. Captain Lewis near falling from the pinnacles of rock 300 feet. He caught himself at 20 feet."

For the first several weeks, the expedition suffered few setbacks. When the wind did not favor sails, the men pushed the boats through the river with oars or with poles pressed against the river bottom.

In addition to their own chores, the men took turns hunting alongside the river. They enjoyed eating fresh game, which also allowed them to conserve the food they had packed for the trip. At night, each man received a small ration of whiskey with his dinner. Pierre "Peter" Cruzatte, one of the privates, brought a fiddle with him. As they drank and ate fresh game, they watched the sun set and listened to the woodsman's music.

Meeting Indians

One of the orders Jefferson had given to the expedition was to try to forge peace among the various Indian tribes they met. However, by mid-July in 1804, the Corps of Discovery had

While traveling up south on the Missouri, Clark spotted tribal markings on rocks similar to ones shown here, which were photographed on rocks in Idaho.

traveled more than five hundred miles without spotting a single Native American. Clark saw tribal markings on rocks, including paintings of human figures, but they still saw no Indians. On July 21, one of the men who had joined the Corps of Discovery in St. Louis, a Private Perry, told Clark that the expedition was just a few miles from a well-known village of the Oto tribe.

On July 28, Drouillard met a Missouri Indian out on the plains. He brought the man back to the base camp. The Indian confirmed to Clark that the tribes in the area—the Otos and the Missouri Indians—were nearby, hunting buffalo on the plains. They would meet them soon.

Over the next several days, Lewis and Clark sent messengers out to find nearby chiefs and invite them to a meeting. On the morning of August 3, 1804, Lewis and Clark held their first formal council with the Indian leaders. They gathered the visiting chiefs from the Oto and Missouri tribes under an awning made from a sail. The sun beat down as the Native Americans watched the enlisted men of the Corps march at arms before them. Lewis and Clark wanted to display the discipline and technology they had as well as impress the chiefs with a sign of strength from the United States.

Chasing Buffalo

Native American tribes that lived along the Missouri River—the Oto, the Missouri, the Yankton, the Dakota and Teton Sioux, and the Mandan—all relied on the buffalo for their survival. They ate buffalo meat, and used the buffalo skins to clothe their bodies and cover their teepees.

Because the buffalo was so important to the various tribes, the Indians moved their entire village in pursuit of the herds, which ranged freely over the prairie. Their teepees were made so that they could be collapsed and carried over great distances as the tribe followed the roaming buffalo.

Sometimes the various Indian tribes fought over the hunting grounds. When Lewis and Clark arrived in the Louisiana Territory, the relationships among all the tribes of the region were tense.

The Indians of the Great Plains all hunted buffalo. They ate its meat and used the animal skins for clothing and to cover their teepees.

When Lewis and Clark came upon a new Indian tribe, they would hold a council meeting like the one pictured here in this 1811 engraving.

After this spectacle, Lewis, with Drouillard translating, delivered a long speech to the chiefs. He explained to them that they now had a "new father"—meaning Jefferson, who came from the "Seventeen great nations"—meaning all the states of the United States as it stood in 1804 and lay to the east. He further explained that the French had now gone across the great waters of the Atlantic Ocean, never to return. If the chiefs wanted their people to prosper, they needed to declare loyalty to the U.S. government and President Thomas Jefferson. After the speech, Lewis distributed gifts of good will to the chiefs. Each man got a peace medal embossed with the face of Jefferson.

If the chiefs wanted their people to prosper, they needed to declare loyalty to the U.S. government and President Thomas Jefferson.

The Indians then took their turn, each man giving a speech to the Americans. Once the exchange of speeches ended, Lewis brought out an **air rifle**, which he had taken along with him, and shot it several times for the chiefs. They were amazed that a gun could show such force and yet it did not smoke or make much noise like the rifles they had acquired—probably from early French and Spanish traders. In addition to the gifts of medals and some food, Lewis then gave the chiefs some gunpowder—not much, the expedition could not spare it—and a bit of whiskey.

Unfortunately, the Indians were not pleased with what they received. They wanted more trade goods—rifles and ammunition, steel, knives, and tools. Lewis tried to explain that they could only offer the token gifts they had presented. The chiefs acted as if they understood, but they still wanted more. From their perspective, here were forty-five white men with a large boat and a handful of pirogues laden with goods, and all they could spare the first tribe they met were trifles.

Lewis then extended an invitation to the Indians to go to Washington, D.C., to meet with President Jefferson. Several chiefs said that they would accept the offer, although none had ever left their homeland. Then the Corps of Discovery and the chiefs parted ways. Lewis and Clark resumed their journey upstream on the river.

Wildlife Along the River

One morning in August, Lewis awoke to see the river coated in a sheet of white feathers. Seventy yards wide and three miles long, the snowy stretch was just one of many natural marvels that the Corps encountered early on in their trip. They followed the river of feathers upstream until they reached a small island. There, Lewis saw a flock of pelicans so large and so dense that he could not even begin to estimate its size. Lewis knew about pelicans from books, but he had never seen any before. They turned the Missouri into an enormous undulating feather bed.

Lewis gathered many species of plants and animals on the journey. Shown here are pressed leaves that he collected.

As they approached, the pelicans took flight. Lewis raised his rifle and shot into the mass of birds. One fell from the sky, and Lewis inspected it carefully. He measured its length, wingspan, and weight. He gutted the bird and inspected the contents of the bird's stomach.

For his part, Lewis preferred to spend most of his time studying and examining the flora and fauna (plants and animals) in his new surroundings. While Clark concerned himself with the logistics of travel, commanding the men on the boats, navigating, and mapmaking, Lewis busily collected samples of birds and plants—of which there were plenty.

Although they did not come across any wooly mammoths or other ancient animals, hardly a week passed without encountering a beast that defied definition. They once spotted fast-running, horned animals racing across the grass. Clark called them a kind of goat. We now know they were a type of antelope. The men of the expedition soon discovered that along with being graceful and fast, these "goats" were also good to eat.

A Second Council Meeting

On August 19, 1804, the expedition planned another council with the local chiefs. Some had participated at the earlier meeting while others were appearing for the first time. Before the council gathered, one of the Indian leaders named Chief Big Horse had presented himself to Lewis and Clark in the morning—stark naked. He intended to show the captains that he and his tribe were very poor and needed goods and other help from the expedition. Unfortunately, this gesture did not generate sympathy but made Clark mildly angry. The incident set the tone for the day.

The pronghorn antelope was among the many animals that Lewis and Clark discovered throughout their journey.

Once more Lewis and Clark met with all the chiefs in the afternoon. The same speech given at the first council was repeated. This time, the chiefs indicated that they would accept the leadership of Jefferson, but they were also eager to trade with the people of America. Then, as before, gifts were handed out to them. Some received medals of peace, while others received certificates that marked their new friendship with the United States.

Not satisfied with the token gifts, the chiefs begged for a barrel of whiskey. Lewis and Clark refused to give them a whole barrel and instead gave each man a ceremonial drink. Lewis again displayed his air rifle and followed up with a demonstration of a magnifying glass. None of the Indians were happy or impressed.

Nevertheless, in accordance with Jefferson's mandate, Lewis and Clark were at least successful in eliciting a promise from the various chiefs to make peace among all the tribes.

Nevertheless, in accordance with Jefferson's mandate, Lewis and Clark were at least successful in eliciting a promise from the various chiefs to make peace among all the tribes. However, they were warned that the Omaha tribe was not represented and that the chiefs could not be sure that a peace would hold.

CHAPTER 6

The Sioux Nation

The [Sioux] is a Stout bold looking people, (the young men handsom[e]) & well made.
　—William Clark

At the time of Lewis and Clark's journey, the Sioux Indians were considered masters of the Missouri River. Made up of several different tribes, the braves, or young warriors, of the Sioux Nation were excellent horsemen and hunters. Reputed to be fierce warriors, they enjoyed the power and influence that they had and would not readily give it up to any group—white or Indian.

Having some knowledge of the Sioux Indians, the expedition was anxious at the possibility of meeting them. However, their encounters with the Sioux would be very different from the meetings they had with the Missouri and Oto tribes.

The Sioux were among the most powerful plains tribes. In this c. 1910 print, Sioux braves battle the Blackfeet tribe.

The Vast Sioux Nation

During the time of the expedition, the entire Sioux Nation included approximately twenty thousand people. Within that broader nation were three main branches called the Dakota, the Teton, also known as Lakota, and the Yankton. These three branches were further divided into many individual tribes, among them the Assiniboine, the Oglata, the Wahpekute, and the Stoney.

All these tribes shared a root language and a **nomadic** lifestyle. They traveled on horseback and ranged across almost the entire area we now know as the **Great Plains**. Because of the size of the Sioux Nation and its nomadic ways, they influenced many tribes in the plains region.

The Sioux language was spoken across a wide range of territory—stretching from what is now Mississippi into Canada. Even non-Sioux tribes in this area spoke similar languages, which are now called Siouan, meaning that they are based on much of the same grammar and vocabulary—much like Spanish, Italian, and Portuguese are all based on Latin.

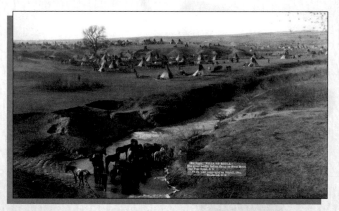

This photograph from the late 1800s by western photographer John Grabill shows a typical Lakota village.

Meeting the Dakota Sioux

A thick fog skimmed along the Missouri on the morning of August 30, 1804. Lewis and Clark peered across the river, into the mist, straining to see the Indians they would soon meet—the Dakota Sioux. Once again, the expedition made preparations for a council and sent one man across the river to invite the chiefs over.

When the fog finally burned off, the chiefs crossed the river at noon, adorned "with paint, porcupine quills, large leggings and moccasins—all with buffalo robes of different colors." Lewis and Clark gathered their guests beneath the shade of an oak tree, an American flag flapping in the breeze above them. Following Lewis's standard speech, Clark gave each chief a medal. One chief, seemingly chosen at random, was declared the Grand Chief by Lewis and Clark and was given a flag, as well as a hat and a European-style jacket. Lewis and Clark sat smoking the peace pipe with the chiefs until supper. So far, they had found all the Indians they met to be friendly enough. That would soon change.

This photograph shows a Lakota brave, as he would have dressed in the early 1900s. At the time Lewis and Clark met his tribe, he would have worn the breastplate and armband.

Danger Among the Lakota Sioux

On September 23 as the Corps of Discovery camped alongside a creek that fed into the Missouri, three Sioux boys approached from the opposite side of the creek. They informed the members of the expedition that two large bands of Lakota Sioux were camped nearby. Clark gave the boys some tobacco with instructions to take it to their chiefs as a gift and invite them to a meeting the next day.

Lewis and Clark gathered gifts for the Lakota in preparations for friendship. They also prepared "all things for action in case of necessity." Although they had done this for each of the previous meetings, no action had been necessary. This meeting with the Lakota Sioux would be different.

While council preparations were being readied, one of the expedition members went off by horse to hunt for elk. He left his horse behind for a bit while he stalked an elk through the brush. Seeing an opportunity, a young Indian stole his horse. The crew member returned to camp and reported the theft.

Later, five young Lakota pulled ashore where Clark was waiting. He told the boys that his group would not meet with their tribe until they returned the horse. "We [are] friends," Clark said. But, "We're not afraid of any Indians."

It is not clear from Clark's journal if the horse was indeed returned, but given what was at stake—the stature and power of the Corps of Discovery—we can assume that it was, which explains why the meeting went forward the following day.

At eleven o'clock the next morning, a group of chiefs approached the camp. This time, they exchanged gifts before the formal meeting. Regrettably, Drouillard, the Corps' primary translator, did not speak the Lakota dialect, so he resorted to sign language. Without a good interpreter, Lewis cut his speech short. Then, he invited three of the chiefs back to the keelboat for a drink of whiskey.

The corpsmen paddled the chiefs out to the keelboat. The chiefs remained on board for three hours, drinking whiskey, and soon, they appeared to be drunk. Clark and Lewis decided it was time to return them to the camp. Clark and the chiefs got back into a pirogue and paddled to the shore. Lewis remained on the keelboat with the rest of the men in the expedition.

Clark landed the pirogue, and the chiefs climbed out onto the sand. Clark tried to push off from shore to return to the keelboat. However, the Lakota would not let him leave. One brave grabbed onto the rope at the bow of the boat, while another hugged the mast. Even without an interpreter, Clark knew they wanted to keep the pirogue. Surrounded by the tribesmen, he began to fear for his life. He drew his sword and shouted to Lewis on the keelboat.

Even without an interpreter, Clark knew they wanted to keep the pirogue.

Lewis ordered all men to take up their firearms. They aimed their cannon and all the rifles at the Lakota. Lewis stood ready to give the order to fire. Knowing he would not be understood, Clark still shouted, "My soldiers are good. I have more medicine [weapons, power] on my boat than I need to kill twenty nations of yours in a single day."

Seeing the weapons pointed at them, the chief ordered his men to release the pirogue, but he asked that the expedition travel upstream to his village, so that the women and children could see the keelboat and meet the members of the expedition. Clark agreed.

This incident was a critical test for Lewis and Clark. If Clark had let the Lakota take the pirogue or handle him roughly, it would have invited the Lakota to take everything the expedition had. If they had opened fire with everything they had, every member of the Lakota tribe, numbering between two and three thousand, would have attacked the Corps of Discovery with everything *they* had. Lewis and Clark had survived this crucial confrontation.

"Guests" of the Lakota Sioux

In a gesture of good will or in a show of power, Clark and the chiefs returned to the keelboat. They sailed a mile upriver and anchored for the night just below an island in the middle of the river. As the crew awakened, rows of Indians crowded against the shore of the river. The ranks of Lakota stretched as far as they could see.

Lewis went ashore with five men to meet some of the Indians who had gathered. He declared them friendly. After having met the tribe separately—first Lewis and then Clark—they were each brought to the largest teepee in camp and wrapped in buffalo robes. Swan feathers covered the floor of the teepee where they smoked and ate with their hosts.

After the food was cleared away, a large fire was made in the center of a circle. Ten musicians came out of the crowd. Some played drums made from skins stretched across hoops. The singing and dancing continued until midnight.

After another day of the Lakota dancing and singing, Clark and Lewis grew tired. They announced that they wanted to

This c. 1905 photograph shows several Sioux chiefs in front of their tepees. Their ornate clothing was meant as a reflection of their power.

return to the keelboat. Some of the chiefs returned to the keelboat with them to spend the night. As they reached the keelboat, the men briefly lost control of the pirogue and paddled over the anchor line, cutting the keelboat loose.

The keelboat spun in the current. Clark shouted for all men to grab their oars and steady the keelboat. The Lakota chiefs heard Clark's yells, and in the confusion, they let out a war cry. Almost instantly, two hundred Lakota tribesmen ran to the shore of the river, most armed with bows and arrows, some with rifles and muskets. They aimed their weapons on the crewmen.

Taking swift action, Lewis and Clark quickly calmed the chiefs and made them understand that they had yelled because their boat was being swept downstream. The chiefs ordered their braves to leave the shore, but sixty remained overnight, to stand watch over their chiefs and the Corps of Discovery.

A Final Farewell to the Sioux

By the next morning, there were three hundred more Lakota Sioux waiting by the camp. The chiefs wanted Lewis and Clark to stay the night again, but the two friends were determined to get underway. To keep the boat from sailing, a chief ordered his men to grab the ropes tied to the bow of the boat, then he demanded more gifts from the party.

Lewis announced that he would not be forced to give anything to anyone. Clark proceeded to aim the small cannon at the Indians holding the ropes. He was prepared to meet violence with violence, but he also knew he had to give himself and his crew a way out of this confrontation. Instead of firing, he tossed some tobacco at the chief, and Lewis did the same. With that, the chief told his men to release the line. The expedition quickly set sail upriver, finally leaving this band of Lakota Sioux behind.

CHAPTER 7

Fort Mandan

Customs & the habits of those people has
[accustomed] [them] to bare more Cold than I
thought it possible for man to endure.
—William Clark

With winter approaching, the Corps of Discovery
needed to find a safe place to wait out the frigid winter
weather. Acting on the advice of the fur traders they had
met in St. Louis, Lewis and Clark made their way north
to the villages of the Mandan Indians, located along the
Missouri River, near what is now Bismarck, North Dakota.
The village had long been the center of the Plains Indian
culture. Tribes from all across the Louisiana Territory
traveled there to trade horses, furs, and tools. This in
turn drew fur traders from English and French companies
to trade there with the Native Americans.

The area offered everything the Corps needed, so they
built a wooden stockade nearby, and called it Fort Mandan.
There, the expedition could
rely on the traders to
translate the local language
for them. Because most of
the traders were French, the

This modern photograph shows a
reconstruction of Fort Mandan,
where the Corps wintered in
1804–1805. The original stockade
encampment burned down the
year after they left it.

language often had to be translated twice—first from the tribal languages of Hidatsa or Mandan into French, then from French into English for Lewis and Clark. Usually expedition members Cruzatte or Drouillard made the French translation.

Sacagawea Joins the Expedition

A week and a half after the expedition arrived at the Mandan villages, one of the French fur traders presented himself to Lewis and Clark. His name was Toussaint Charbonneau. He offered his services as an interpreter and guide for the Corps of Discovery.

Born in Canada, Charbonneau had traveled across the northern territories as a fur trader and trapper, so he knew the lay of the land. Having spent most of his life on the wild frontiers, he also had skills as a woodsman. Unfortunately, he had a tendency to stretch the truth. He told Lewis and Clark that he could speak several Indian languages. Although he spoke Mandan passably well, his knowledge of the tongues spoken by tribes upstream was later shown to be almost nonexistent. He told the men that he could handle a boat, which ultimately turned out to be a disastrous exaggeration.

His greatest asset was his pregnant sixteen-year-old Shoshone Indian bride, Sacagawea. She grew up in the Rocky Mountains until the age of twelve or thirteen, when a band of Blackfeet Indians attacked her village and took her as a slave. They traded Sacagawea from one band to another, until finally Charbonneau either bought her as a slave-wife or won her in a game of chance. Now she found herself five months pregnant and preparing to travel west again—this time with a band of white men. For the next stage of the expedition, Sacagawea would be the true interpreter and guide for the Corps of Discovery.

When Lewis and Clark met Toussaint Charbonneau, they hired him as a translator. However, his young wife, Sacagawea, proved to be the better interpreter.

A Frigid Winter

On Christmas day in 1804, the men awoke early and began firing their rifles in the air to celebrate the holiday. The shots roused Clark, who quickly got into the spirit of things and ordered the men to fire the cannon three times. He gave each man a glass of brandy, and for Christmas dinner, they all ate fresh buffalo meat with some dried fruits for dessert.

The cold that blasted across the plains was like nothing any of the men had felt before.

Over the preceding weeks, the temperature plummeted to forty degrees below zero Fahrenheit. The cold that blasted across the plains was like nothing any of the men had felt before.

On February 11, Sacagawea went into labor. It was her first child, and because she was a small woman, the birth was a difficult one. Luckily, with the help of a Frenchman, she gave birth to a baby boy, Jean Baptiste, who was nicknamed Pompey.

The Birth of Pompey

When Sacagawea went into labor in February of 1805, one of the Frenchmen staying with the expedition acted as a **midwife** to the Indian girl. In order to induce a quicker, easier birth, he resorted to a Native American remedy. He asked Lewis for the rattle of a rattlesnake. The man ground up a portion of the rattle and mixed it with water. He fed the mixture to Sacagawea with his fingers. Ten minutes later, "a fine boy"—Jean Baptiste Charbonneau—was born. Lewis admitted that the strange remedy seemed to work, but the notion of giving a pregnant woman a portion of a poisonous snake still bewildered him. Jean Baptiste, or Pompey as Clark would nickname him, became the youngest member of the Corps of Discovery as they traveled westward.

Sacagawea's newborn baby boy, Jean Baptiste, would become the youngest member of the expedition.

Spring came slowly to the northern plains. Temperatures crept upward in March and April as scattered stands of cottonwood began to show hints of green. However, the true sign of spring at Fort Mandan was the Missouri River itself. In late March, the river's ice skin collapsed under its own weight. But the water flowing beneath it had slowed to a trickle. Somewhere upstream an ice dam was blocking almost all of the snowmelt, keeping it from flowing downriver. On March 30, the ice dam gave way, blasting a torrent of water, giant chunks of ice, and dead buffalo—caught in the river's onslaught—downstream. Clark watched as the Mandan leapt onto ice chunks, snagged the carcasses of drowned buffalo from the water, and dragged the soggy corpses to the shore for food.

Spring was here, and it was time for Lewis and Clark to move on.

The Keelboat Returns Home

The men had spent the previous weeks preparing the boats for travel. From this point, the party would split in two. The keelboat was to be loaded with maps, reports, Native American artifacts, and samples of plants and animals for President Jefferson. The cargo would all be sent back to St. Louis with several members of the expedition accompanying it. Everyone else would continue upriver in six small canoes—which were acquired along the way—and two larger pirogues.

Lewis packed the keelboat carefully. He crated all the items and included a list of the contents in every crate. The shipment included the following curiosities: male and female antelope skeletons, the horns of two mule deer, a Mandan bow and a quiver of arrows, four horns of the mountain ram, or big horn sheep, a cage containing what Lewis called a living, burrowing squirrel of the prairies (prairie dog), a cage of four magpies, and a cage containing one living prairie hen.

When Lewis and Clark discovered the prairie dog, they first described it as a type of squirrel.

Over the winter, Lewis and Clark had spent a lot of time talking to Mandan and Hidatsa tribesmen who said they had traveled as far as the Rocky Mountains and back again. Clark tried his best to take the information he got from these interviews and incorporate it into the maps he was drawing for the trip.

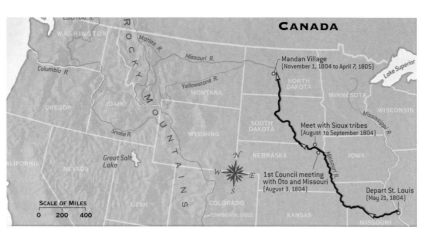

The Corps of Discovery left St. Louis on May 21, 1804. In its first summer, it traveled one thousand miles up the Missouri River and met various Indian tribes along the way. During their first winter, the Corps wintered at Fort Mandan in what is now North Dakota.

Although he now had a clear picture of the Missouri River valley between St. Louis and Fort Mandan, the maps resulting from discussions with the Mandan were merely crude guidelines for the journey west.

As the keelboat began its journey back downstream to St. Louis, the rest of the expedition said good-bye to their friends, the Mandan. Lewis, Clark, and all their crew pushed off from the shore and set off toward the West. Their number was now reduced to thirty-three. Among them were thirty-one men, one woman—Sacagawea, and her child—Jean Baptiste.

The White Bear

Earlier in the journey, the men heard stories of a ferocious animal that the Indians called the white bear. Today we know it as a grizzly bear. Armed with rifles, the men of the expedition were excited to meet this monster. Perhaps a bit cocky, they figured the bear would be an easy prey to their guns.

On April 29, 1805, Lewis had his first encounter with such a creature. Walking on shore with some other men, they came across two bears lumbering by the riverside. They took aim and shot. One bear escaped, but the other one, now wounded, chased after Lewis. He said that this bear was "more furious and formidable" than the eastern black bear, but he still figured, "in the hands of [skillful] riflemen they are by no means as formidable or dangerous as they have been represented."

The following week, Clark and Drouillard killed another grizzly bear. Despite the bear's incredible life force, Lewis still thought grizzly hunting was just good sport. He wrote, "I expect these gentlemen will give us some amusement shortly."

Several days later, one of the men shot a grizzly, but it did not die. He ran to find Lewis and the other men who stalked and finally killed the bear after shooting it five times. After all of these bear run-ins, Lewis finally had to confess, "I do not like the gentlemen and had [rather] fight two Indians than one bear."

Lewis and Clark, depicted in this painting from 1904, had heard stories about the grizzly bear and were anxious to meet with one, but they quickly learned hunting these animals was a fearful and dangerous job.

The Pirogue Accident

By mid-May, the Corps of Discovery had traveled 2,200 miles with many more to go. Drouillard normally handled the rudder of the pirogue, which carried in its hull all the records of the expedition's journey, including their papers, navigational instruments, maps, and journals. To lose any of them would make further progress on the river almost impossible.

Sadly, on this evening, Charbonneau held the rudder. He feared the water and had little boating experience. Lewis described him as "perhaps the most timid waterman in the world."

Suddenly a powerful wind kicked up. Charbonneau panicked and turned the rudder the wrong way. The pirogue rolled onto its side, nearly dumping its precious cargo into the river. Water poured over the edge of the hull. Fearful, Charbonneau released the rudder entirely, and the boat was about to overturn completely. Cruzatte, one of the men on board, threatened to shoot Charbonneau if he did not take hold of the rudder immediately and right the boat. Charbonneau finally got control of himself and righted the boat.

During the confusion of her husband's blunder, Sacagawea remained calm and carefully reached into the water to collect the crucial papers and light articles that had washed overboard. Once the boat was steadied, they paddled across the river and onto the shore. The men spent the next morning drying the contents of the pirogue by the side of the river. For Sacagawea's quick action, Lewis later wrote, "I ascribe equal fortitude and resolution, with any person on board at the time of the [accident]."

A modern painting depicts Toussaint Charbonneau, who overstated his own abilities to handle a boat and to translate.

CHAPTER 8

Finding the Great Falls

An interesting question was now to be determined;
which of these rivers was the Missouri.
        —Meriwether Lewis

On the evening of June 3, 1805, the Corps of Discovery set up camp at a fork in the river. One fork ran somewhat northward with mud darkening its waters. Another fork ran in a southwesterly direction. Its waters were clear and fast moving. Which was the true Missouri?

Although the Mandan Indians had told them that the Missouri ran for miles in the Rocky Mountains, they had not mentioned a fork like this one. Tribe members had also told them of a landmark along the Missouri, which they called the Great Falls.

Lewis thought the south fork was the true Missouri. He argued that a river running from the Rocky Mountains would likely be fast and clear. The other men did not agree. The muddy water of the northern fork resembled the Missouri River they had thus far traveled upon.

There was only one way to determine which river was the actual Missouri. They would follow one of the forks. Lewis took a small group of men along the north fork on foot. On June 8, Lewis determined that it went too far north to be the Missouri River. He named this tributary (a river that flows into a larger river) the Marias River in honor of his cousin Maria Wood. They would explore the Marias River more thoroughly on the return trip.

This painting shows Lewis and Clark with the Corps of Discovery at the fork of the Marias River and the Missouri River.

Discovering the Falls

After returning from the north fork, now called the Marias River, Lewis still could not fully convince the rest of the Corps of Discovery that it was not the Missouri River. In order to ensure that they were on the correct path, Lewis decided to travel ahead by foot with Drouillard and three others to find the Great Falls as proof. The rest of the expedition would travel more slowly on the river.

Lewis and his small party left on their advance trek and marched for three days. On the morning of June 13, Lewis awoke and started walking, when after two miles he began to hear the unmistakable sound of water falling over stone. He caught a glimpse of some rising mist and ran toward it.

Lewis was awestruck. The Great Falls of the Missouri—actually made up of five separate falls—stood before him. Water washed over the edge of the cliffs and fell at least eighty feet. The foaming basin below the falls churned. In the mist above the falls, a rainbow arched through the air. Lewis tried his best to capture the beauty of the scene in his journal. He wished that he "might be enabled to give to the enlightened world some just idea of this truly [magnificent] and sublimely grand object, which has from the commencement of time been concealed from the view of civilized man."

Having caught some trout in the river, they cooked them with some meat from the buffalo they had hunted earlier. That night they ate happily with the roaring falls in the background.

The next day, Lewis sent one of his men, Joseph Field, back to the expedition with a letter for Clark, asking him to meet them at the falls.

Getting Past the Great Falls

Upon receiving Lewis's letter, the whole expedition proceeded as far as it could upriver in their canoes and pirogues. Upon reaching the falls, they could go no farther. They would have to carry their gear over land for this portion of the trip. They dragged the boats out of the river and stored them far enough from the water's edge so that they would not be swept away in the following spring's floods. To lighten their load, they buried lead and some sealed kegs of powder, along with other materials that they did not need immediately and were too heavy to carry.

This lovely view of the Great Falls shows a section called Rainbow Falls.

The Great Falls of the Missouri

The Great Falls of the Missouri is made up of five separate waterfalls—the Black Eagle Falls (26 feet), Rainbow Falls (47 feet), Crooked Falls (19 feet), the Great Falls (87 feet), and Colter Falls (14 feet). A dam at the Great Falls floods the upstream valley so that Colter Falls is now underwater.

When Lewis and Clark discovered the Great Falls, they also discovered a previously unknown species of fish called the cutthroat trout—the same tasty fish they dined on that first night at the falls. Today, the fish's formal Latin name—*Oncorhynchus clarki lewisi*—honors the explorers.

Lewis and Clark discovered and dined on the cutthroat trout they found swimming in the waters near the Great Falls.

Carrying their load of equipment and cargo, the men trudged to the top and past the falls. This was the point at which they would test Lewis's second boat design. They unpacked the iron frame of the boat. If it worked, it would be a masterstroke. They needed to cover the iron frame with sewn-together elk hides and then seal the seams of the hides with pine-pitch tar to keep the boat from leaking.

There was one problem. They were no pine trees from which to make the tar. Lewis needed to use what was available. He ordered the men to make a concoction of charcoal, bees wax, and bear fat. This, he hoped, would waterproof the boat.

The men proceeded to cover the boat frame with the sewn elk skins. Then they applied the waterproofing compound to the seams and stitches. Lewis admired his handiwork. The large boat was light enough that a handful of men could lift and carry it when empty. Once it was on the water, the boat could hold several thousand pounds of men and cargo—if it did not leak.

Carrying their load of equipment and cargo, the men trudged to the top and past the falls.

It was now July 9. The Corps of Discovery had spent nearly a month in the area, first carrying all their gear past the Great Falls and then waiting for the iron-framed boat to be constructed. Lewis ordered the newly made vessel be set afloat on the water. The hand-made craft looked perfect, bobbing on the water like a cork. To his horror, however, Lewis soon realized the compound of bees wax, charcoal, and bear fat was flaking from the seams of the elk skins, and the boat was leaking like a sieve. Dejected, he gave up on his boat. The men were ordered instead to build canoes from hollowed trees. With all these delays, Lewis wondered if he would be able to cross the Rocky Mountains before winter set in.

When the portable, iron-framed boat failed to work, the men made dugout canoes, hollowing logs with axes as shown.

CHAPTER 9

The Shoshone Tribe

We begin to feel considerable anxiety with respect to the [Shoshone] Indians. If we do not find them or some other nation who have horses I fear the successful issue of our voyage will be very doubtful.
　　—Meriwether Lewis

After loading their new canoes, the men continued on the Missouri River and into the mountains. They found the character of the river changed drastically. The current became swift and the shoreline turned rocky. The dominant vegetation around was a plant called the prickly pear, a cactus. Often, the men had to walk on shore and tow the canoes with ropes against the swift current. The needles of the cactus pierced their moccasins as they stumbled over the stony ground. Everyone walked on bloody, sore feet.

The buffalo were mostly gone now, left behind in the plains below. As they traveled farther into the mountains, they knew that they would soon reach the end of the Missouri. If they had any hope of reaching the other side

The prickly pear cactus covered the path the Corps took. It has a sweet fruit and sharp spines. The spines cut the men's feet as they walked.

of the mountains, they needed to acquire some horses. At Fort Mandan, they had been told that the Shoshone, the tribe of Sacagawea, had horses.

Looking for the Shoshone Tribe

Where were the Shoshone? They saw signs of an Indian tribe by the banks of the river. They passed campsites and abandoned villages, but they did not see or meet any people from the tribe.

Soon Sacagawea began to recognize landmarks along the river and the surrounding hills. She announced that this was the place where her family had lived. It was now early August and even with Sacagawea's hopeful recognition of the area, the situation of the expedition was beginning to look desperate. Half of the men were injured in some way. They could find no game

When the Corps of Discovery approached Sacagawea's childhood home, she recognized the land and river, telling them they were on the right path. She is shown here, pointing the way.

The Shoshone and the Blackfeet

For decades, the Shoshone had suffered at the hands of the Blackfeet Indians. While the Shoshone were fierce warriors, they had no guns at all. The Blackfeet had acquired guns from the British, and they frequently attacked the Shoshone, raiding their horses and taking members of the tribe as slaves. This is how Sacagawea was stolen from her family.

Fearful of the Blackfeet, the Shoshone took shelter in the mountains. If the Blackfeet caught a group of Shoshone braves on their hunting ground, the Blackfeet always attacked them. As a result, the Shoshone were poor and often hungry. They subsisted on the food they could gather in the mountains, making only occasional trips onto the plains to hunt buffalo. It was this fear of the Blackfeet that made the Shoshone so difficult to find.

The Shoshone, shown here on horseback, were famous for their horses. Lewis and Clark needed their help getting across the Rocky Mountains.

to hunt. The river was shallow, and there were many rocky rapids, forcing the men to walk on the uneven ground and pull the canoes behind them.

On August 9, Lewis took two other men, Sergeant Shields and Drouillard, and traveled ahead of the group. Three men hiking could move more quickly and, hopefully, find the Shoshone faster. Once the tribe was found, Lewis could negotiate for the horses.

A Slight Language Problem

On August 11, Lewis spotted his first Shoshone Indian in the far distance. The Indian approached on horseback. When he was a mile away, the Indian brave stopped and eyed the three men warily. Lewis pulled a blanket from his pack, opened it, and then tossed it into the air. This was considered a gesture of friendship. Lewis was inviting the Indian to come and sit with him on the blanket. The Shoshone Indian did not move from his spot.

Lewis picked up his blanket and started walking toward the Indian again. He could see that the man was still frightened. Lewis then shouted, "TAB-BA-BONE!" meaning "white man." Sacagawea had taught him this word a few days earlier. However, the Shoshone had no word for "white men." The word *tab-ba-bone* most closely translated to the Shoshone word for "stranger." And to the Shoshone brave, the word that meant "stranger" also meant "enemy."

On August 11, Lewis spotted his first Shoshone Indian in the far distance.

From the point-of-view of the Shoshone brave, he saw a man walking toward him, smiling, showing signs of friendship. At the same time, that man was yelling "ENEMY!" Lewis rolled up his sleeves to show the white flesh of his arm. He shouted "Tab-ba-bone!" The Indian turned his horse around and rode off into the distance.

Lewis and his men followed, tracking the brave's path for two days, until finally they saw two Shoshone women and a man. Lewis ordered his men to remain behind. He walked toward them, waving a flag. At first, it appeared these Shoshone would wait to meet him. Once again, Lewis shouted, "Tab-ba-bone!" The Indians ran away.

A Shoshone Native American is photographed c. 1900 with a peace pipe. Smoking was an act of relaxation and friendship.

Lewis and his men chased the Shoshone. A mile farther on, they came across three Indian women. One woman fled, but an older woman and a young girl remained behind. Lewis placed his gun on the ground, waved his flag, and walked slowly toward them. The old woman did not run. When Lewis got close, he gave her some gifts—an awl for making moccasins, some beads, and some paint. She now understood that he wanted to be a friend.

Lewis and his men walked another two miles when sixty warriors on horseback came to meet them. Once again, Lewis laid down his gun and walked toward the warriors. He took out a peace pipe and lit it. The warriors understood and approached Lewis to give him an embrace of friendship. Lewis then met the chief, Cameahwait. Together with the Indians, Lewis and his men sat down on the ground and removed their moccasins, an act of sincerity and trust. Then they smoked the peace pipe.

Sacagawea's Reunion

Lewis communicated with the Shoshone tribe using sign language. They carried on simple conversations, but Lewis needed a translator to help him with more complicated issues. He knew Sacagawea, who was a Shoshone, could help but she was with Clark's group, which was following slowly behind. After a few days with the Shoshone, Lewis decided to take Cameahwait and some other Shoshone to find the rest of the Corps of Discovery.

Some of the Shoshone feared Lewis was leading them into an ambush by the Blackfeet Indians. In order to regain their trust, Lewis handed his rifle to Cameahwait and said to him, "If I have deceived you, you may make use of that gun as you think proper." In other words, he was telling Cameahwait to shoot him if Lewis was lying and leading the Shoshone into an ambush. The chief accepted the gun, and understood what Lewis was saying.

On Saturday, August 17, Clark, Charbonneau, and Sacagawea were walking ahead of the main expedition. Several warriors appeared on horseback. Sacagawea recognized their style of dress immediately. They were Shoshone. She shouted with excitement to see members of her own tribe.

This c. 1899 photograph of a Shoshone Indian shows how Cameahwait's tribesmen may have looked and dressed.

Clark, Charbonneau, Sacagawea, and others from the expedition were brought to meet Chief Cameahwait. Sacagawea recognized Cameahwait immediately. He was her brother! They embraced happily. Whatever lingering suspicions Cameahwait had for the white men melted away. After many years of being apart, his sister had returned to him.

When Clark came forward to meet Chief Cameahwait, the young chief gave him one gift that stood out—seashells. Clark knew they must have come from the Pacific Ocean. This was proof that they were on the right path.

Sacagawea is joyfully reunited with her brother Cameahwait, introducing him to his nephew Pompey.

Across the Continental Divide

The next step for the Corps of Discovery was to find a way through the mountains to search for the Columbia River, which they were sure they would find on the other side. After all the struggles the men of the Corps of Discovery had endured, they could not have realized that the most difficult part of their journey was about to begin. They would be trudging through a maze of dense mountains looking for the Columbia while winter closed in rapidly around them. They needed a guide and some horses. The Shoshone had both.

Cameahwait and Lewis and Clark struck a deal for the Corps of Discovery to buy some horses from the Shoshone. They also offered to help guide the Corps of Discovery through the mountains. The Corps needed that help as much as they needed

The Continental Divide

The Rocky Mountains rise more than ten thousand feet above sea level. All the rain and snow that falls on these mountains must flow down the mountains to the sea. The point at which the water flows either eastward or westward down the mountain is called the Continental Divide. The water traveling east has a gradual descent. From this part of the mountains, it flows down the Missouri River, into the Mississippi River, and into the Gulf of Mexico. The water flowing west has a much more rapid descent to sea level because the distance to the Pacific Ocean from the Rockies is much shorter. Thus, the water crashes down, creating furious rapids. On August 21, Lewis crossed the divide for the first time at a spot now called the Lemhi Pass. Looking west, he saw snow-capped mountains.

A narrow road cuts through the Lemhi Pass in this modern photograph of the point where Lewis and Clark crossed the Continental Divide and saw mountain ranges to the west.

the horses. At this point the Corps of Discovery was crossing the Continental Divide. The divide is an invisible line that runs through the highest part of the Rocky Mountain range. Because the territory is so high, the weather changes quickly between seasons. On August 21, the height of summer in most places, Lewis awoke to find ice on the river and the ink in his pen frozen.

It was decided that Clark should go ahead of the main group with an Indian guide named Old Toby to see what was ahead. As Old Toby led Clark up a river valley, the path narrowed and stony mountains rose steeply on both sides of the river, now churning white water. Clark could see that the expedition could not easily pass alongside the canyon on horses, and they would not be able to advance upstream in canoes. Clark had hoped he would find an easy pass through the mountains to the Columbia River, where the men could then build canoes and float downstream to the Pacific. However, looking at the scene before him, he realized getting over the mountain range would not be easy. He wrote a letter to Lewis and sent it back with the Indian guide. Lewis would need to buy more horses.

Once Lewis received Clark's letter, he began bargaining with Cameahwait for more horses. Knowing that the expedition desperately needed the animals, the chief and his people drove hard bargains. Clark later returned to the camp. He joined the bargaining discussions, reminding Cameahwait that if his people assisted them, they would make sure that the U.S. government

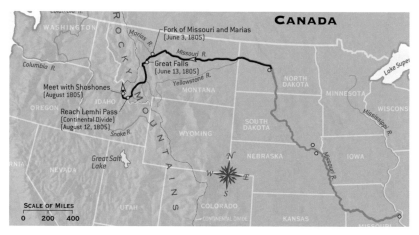

Upon leaving Fort Mandan, the expedition came to a fork in the Missouri. Lewis named the tributary the Marias River. In June 1805, Lewis found the Great Falls. Traveling through the Rocky Mountains, the Corps reached the Continental Divide and met Sacagawea's tribe, the Shoshone.

Lewis and Clark are pictured on horseback riding through the treacherous Rocky Mountains.

helped the tribe. Still the prices were steep. The next day Clark traded a gun for a horse. The Corps had a policy against giving guns to Indians, but they needed the horses.

A Long and Winding Path

On August 30, the Corps of Discovery, including Sacagawea, set out, leaving behind Cameahwait and most of his tribe. They would travel north over a mountain pass. Travel became very difficult almost immediately. The horses stumbled on the steep rocky paths. Several slipped and tumbled down the mountainside. By the second day, one horse was crippled and two others collapsed from exhaustion.

Cold, wet, and hungry, the men continued over the hard path through snow and sleet. They reached the village of the Flathead Indian tribe. Although the members of this tribe had never met white men before, they greeted the expedition with warmth and generosity. They also sold eleven good horses to Lewis and Clark at a fair price.

With fresh horses, the men continued their journey deeper into the mountains. They finally reached a creek that Lewis dubbed Traveler's Rest Creek. There, Old Toby told Lewis something surprising. He said that men on horseback could have taken a short cut and reached the same point in four days rather than the fifty-two days it took them by following the Missouri. Lewis must have been upset. They had wasted so much time. On the return trip, they would check out this short cut. For now, the expedition would continue their climb.

Worried, and now standing from a high vantage point, Clark looked out and saw "high rugged mountains in every direction as far as I could see." It was also bitterly cold as Clark wrote, "I have been wet and as cold in every part as I ever was in my life." He worried that his feet would literally freeze. The group would now start its trip down the mountains.

> "I have been wet and as cold in every part as I ever was in my life."

By the middle of September, the men had all but run out of food, so Clark and six men descended from the barren mountains ahead of the rest of the Corps of Discovery. They left behind meat they had hunted so that Lewis and the larger group would have food as they came down from the mountains.

As the exhausted expedition members reached flat land, they must have all felt a sense of triumph as they saw a flat green plain opened up before them. Finally, their horses could stride comfortably across the ground and graze on the grassland.

Clark and his men then continued westward for three easy miles when they came to an Indian village, home to the Nez Percé tribe.

CHAPTER 10

Journey Down the Rapids

Lewis scarcely able to ride on a [gentle] horse which was furnished by the chief, Several men [were] So unwell that they were compelled to lie on the Side of the road for some time.

—William Clark

The Nez Percé Indians had met few white men before, but they welcomed Clark's group with food and fed them salmon, berries, and onion-like roots. Unaccustomed to the strange food, the men became sick almost immediately after eating.

Lewis and the rest of the expedition joined Clark a few days later. Like the first bunch, the men came down with stomach pains and sickness. After weeks of near starvation in the mountains, this illness could have been fatal as no one could keep much food down. Lewis became so sick he could not ride a horse.

Lewis became so sick he could not ride a horse.

Although sick himself, Clark distributed dozens of Rush's pills to the men, but this may have been the worst possible medicine under the circumstances. They needed something to settle their stomachs, and Rush's pills were intended to flush out the digestive system.

Most of the men guessed that the fish and the roots had made them ill. In order to get some meat that suited

This Nez Percé Indian, photographed in 1910, is dressed as his great grandfather would have been when Lewis and Clark arrived at their village.

them better, they began purchasing dogs from the Nez Percé to eat. Although Clark never grew fond of dog meat, Lewis would later admit that he found dog meat to be just as tasty and nutritious as any buffalo meat.

Today, historians still disagree over what caused the men to become ill. Many believe that the fish contained bacteria that the Nez Percé Indians were immune to but were harmful to the men of the expedition who were not accustomed to it. Others believe that the men had picked up an illness from the Shoshone that did not manifest itself until the expedition had reached the Nez Percé tribe.

Preparing for the River Journey

The men lingered with the Nez Percé for days as they tried to get their strength back. During this time, Clark and Lewis started to prepare for the next leg of the journey. Their horses, so desperately procured just a month earlier, were now useless to them. The rest of the trip would be on water flowing downriver to the ocean. Because they would be leaving the horses with the Nez Percé over the winter, Clark had the men brand the horses, to indicate they were the owners. The expedition would then pick up the herd the following spring on their way back home.

Instead of horses, the expedition now needed canoes. The men would have to make them out of the trees found in the area.

Making Canoes

The main type of canoe used by the Corps of Discovery was called a dugout canoe. To make one, the men cut down a tree that had a long, straight trunk. Using axes, they shaped the trunk of the tree and hollowed out the inside, making the canoe buoyant (floatable) and creating a place to sit and space to store their supplies. At that time, most Indian tribes did not have steel axes, so they hollowed out the canoe by setting small fires along its length and then scraped out the burned wood.

The advantage to a dugout canoe was its availability. If there were large trees around, the men could make as many canoes as needed. The downside was that they were very heavy and hard to handle. They also rolled over—or capsized—easily when in rough waters.

A 1590 colored engraving shows how ancient Native Americans made dugout canoes without any steel tools. They built small fires along the logs they cut down, then scraped the burned wood out to hollow the log.

The men of the Corps of Discovery are depicted making canoes from felled trees. The heavy dugout canoes would carry them to the ocean.

They adopted the techniques of the Indian tribes around them and improved on those techniques when they could.

The men finished their canoes quickly and launched the first two on October 5 to see how they would handle in the water. One leaked a bit. By evening, two more canoes were finished and set into the water. Clark wrote that they "proved to be [very] good." In honor of the place they had made their canoes, the men named the area Canoe Camp.

Racing Downriver

After final preparations, the Corps of Discovery was on the move again on October 7, 1805. They were paddling down the Clearwater River in what is now the state of Idaho. Eventually the Clearwater would enter the Snake River, which was a major tributary of the Columbia River—the waterway that would take them to the Pacific Ocean.

They quickly met the fast-flowing rapids. Late on October 8, Sergeant Gass was steering a canoe when it struck a rock. The canoe turned over. Water rushed into it. This was one of the larger canoes, and it held several men. As hard as it is to believe, most of them could not swim. They clung to the canoe while it swirled in the current. The cargo spilled into the river. Clark ordered the other canoes to pluck the men and the gear from the water. Wet and shaken, the men dried out over night and then set out again the following day with one less canoe.

The Corps of Discovery traveled down the rapids on their way to the Pacific. Some of the canoes capsized and sank.

Over the next several days, the men would again shoot through rapids and swamp their canoes, filling them with water. Clark recognized the danger, both to the men and to the supplies. On October 11, he wrote that they should have carried the canoes around the rapids on land, a practice called *portaging*. However, days were racing past them. It was nearly mid-October. Lewis and Clark were intent on reaching the Pacific before winter. They had no way of knowing what the weather would be like as the seasons changed and they did not want to be caught part way to the ocean when winter arrived in full force. Therefore, they took risks.

When the Corps of Discovery reached portions of the river they could not pass through, they portaged, hauling their canoes and gear over land as is shown in this painting.

On the Columbia River

On October 16, the expedition, now traveling on the Snake River, arrived at a fork. They had finally reached the Columbia River—although they probably thought they had been traveling on it all this time. The current of the Columbia drove them downstream at a pace of thirty miles a day. Compared to their creeping rate through the mountains, this speed was absolutely dizzying.

They traveled quickly despite the change in the weather. Near-desert conditions prevailed through the Rocky Mountains. Now, in the lowlands, fog and rain became the dominant

The Corps raced downstream on the Columbia River in their canoes but stopped often to dry their goods or simply rest. This painting depicts a stop along the route.

conditions. Dense forests grew along the river. By early November, the fog was so thick that Lewis "could not see a man 50 steps off." The wildlife changed as well. They began to see seabirds, gulls, and storks. Sea otters, with their beautiful and valuable skins, played in the river.

On November 4, the expedition landed at a large Chinook Indian village of huts made from wood with thatched roofs. Lewis counted fifty-two canoes on the shore by the village. When the men entered the village, they were welcomed with roots and potatoes to eat.

Another group of Indians from an upstream village arrived not long after the Corps of Discovery did. This tribe came, Lewis supposed, "for the purpose . . . of paying us a friendly visit." This tribe, however, did not present a friendly face. The men were armed, both with traditional Indian weapons as well as with muskets and pistols. The Corps of Discovery stayed on its guard.

While the weapons of these Indians made Lewis and Clark uneasy, their clothes made them hopeful. The Indians dressed in European garb—sailor jackets, overalls, and blue blankets. To Lewis and Clark, this was another sign that the expedition was getting very close to the ocean, for they thought the tribe must

The Corps of Discovery met with Chinook Indians living along the Columbia River. This c. 1910 photograph shows a Chinook standing on the banks of the Columbia, where they made their living.

have surely acquired their weapons and clothes from a ship that had stopped nearby.

Seeing the Ocean at Last!

The expedition continued to make good time even though it rained almost constantly. They slowed long enough to meet with other Chinook Indian tribes along the way, but they still logged as many as thirty-four miles a day. They were close now, they could literally taste it. The river water had turned salty.

On November 7, 1805, the river opened up wide. It was at this point that Clark wrote his famous entry "Oh [ocean] in view! O! The joy!" They were in the mouth of the Columbia River now, twenty miles from the open ocean. The spirits of all the men soared. They had traveled four thousand miles from their starting point in St. Louis. A year and a half of hard work and struggle was now rewarded with an overwhelming sense of accomplishment. Now they needed to find a safe place to stay for the winter.

Though it would be several days more before any members of the expedition saw the open ocean, they felt its effects directly. While trying to camp by the north side of the mouth of the Columbia, Lewis and Clark forgot to account for the tides that would raise water levels near their site. Rain and storms kept them pinned down at their campsite by

In 2005, the United States Mint commemorated the journey of Lewis and Clark with this nickel inscribed with Clark's famous words from his field journal: "Ocean in view! O! The joy!"

the edge of the water. On November 9, a raging storm blew in, flooding their camp. All the men scrambled to secure the canoes before the waves washed them away. Everyone was "as wet as water could make them" all through the night and into the next day. Their clothes and blankets began to rot. Still, the mood of the expedition did not sour. Lewis went out with a few men to find a new camp more protected from the ocean's wrath.

Lewis and Clark are shown in this image with their crew and several local Indians at the winter camp by the ocean. Note the peaked hats worn by the Clatsop Indians, which kept the rain off their heads.

CHAPTER 11

Fort Clatsop

O! [horrible] is the day waves braking with great violence against the shore throwing the water into our Camp.
—William Clark

The miserable weather continued as they held up on the northern edge of the bay, near the present day city of Astoria, Oregon. They were quickly becoming familiar with the rainy weather that the region is famous for. Over the next several days, Lewis and Clark each took turns exploring the area, but their dugout canoes were ill suited for the wind-driven waves that swept across the bay. The swells rolled them over and swamped them so easily that the men tried loading stones in the bottom of the canoes to steady them. The joy that the men had previously felt was giving way to despair.

Members of the Clatsop tribe visited the expedition. They came across the bay in canoes that were designed for these waters. Their crafts cut through the chop of the waves and remained upright. Lewis and Clark bought three canoes from the Clatsop and sought their advice on where the Corps of Discovery should spend the winter.

Lewis and Clark replaced the heavy low canoes, like the one shown here, with canoes they bought from the Clatsop Indians that were more stable in the waters of the bay.

Elk, like this one, supplied food for the men through the winter at Fort Clatsop. They also provided the men with skins for clothes and moccasins.

The Clatsop told them that if they moved across the bay, near their village, they would find more protection from the weather. There they would also find elk—"easier to kill and better meat" than deer, to Clark's thinking. The elk also offered larger, tougher skins that the men could tan and use to replace their rotting clothes and moccasins. It was also clear that the Clatsop Indians had regular contact with trading ships that came into the bay. If a ship arrived while the men were there, they might even be able to sail home.

Before making the decision to move to the southern side of the bay, Lewis and Clark had all the members of the party, including York and Sacagawea, vote on it. The vote was nearly unanimous. They would cross the bay, hoping to find better food, some protection from the driving wind, and perhaps a friendly ship. In the course of history, something greater may have happened here than just the decision to seek shelter on the other side of the bay. This moment is widely regarded as the first time in American history that a woman, Sacagawea, and a black man, York, voted in an election.

Building Winter Quarters

Sadly, the south shore of the bay did not meet expectations. The weather worsened. A gale blew through that was so strong, Clark thought it would uproot trees around them. While the temperatures were mild compared to what they experienced the previous winter at Fort Mandan, the rain soaked into everything they owned. Work on building their winter quarters went slowly.

Fort Clatsop, as they named it, took a month to complete. In the meantime, the men were at the mercy of the wind and the rain. When finished on December 30, 1805, the fort was fifty feet square, with a stockade wall around it. Within the spiked walls of the stockade were seven cabins for the men. Each cabin had a fireplace near the center. They constructed a gate to close off the camp and established regular night watch duties for all the men.

This reconstruction of Fort Clatsop shows the gate to the fort as well as the cabins constructed for the men.

Meriwether Lewis, shown here with his dog Seaman, kept careful notes through most of the journey.

Christmas came without any real celebration. On the previous holiday in 1804, Lewis and Clark handed out whiskey to all the men. This year, the whiskey was all gone. They passed out twists of tobacco to the men who smoked or chewed. The others received small gifts from the diminishing stock of gifts intended for the Indians. New Year's Day was even more lackluster. The men marked the arrival of 1806 by shooting their rifles into the air early in the morning. They dined on elk, *wappetoe* (a type of potato), and water. Lewis, perhaps trying to keep his spirits up, looked forward to New Year's 1807, "when in the bosom of our friends we hope to participate in the mirth and hilarity of the day, and . . . [recollect] the present."

Life at Fort Clatsop

Lewis and Clark each busied themselves with their clerical tasks throughout the winter. Lewis, who had written little in the journals over the fall, threw himself into his writing. He made careful notes of all the birds and animals that he saw along the bay. The sea otters and seals got special attention both because they were beautiful and because he knew they had economic value for their skins.

Clark spent the winter at Fort Clatsop finalizing a map of their journey. This re-creation, both beautiful and precise, shows the rough terrain they covered.

Clark studied all the smaller maps he had made across the country then combined them into one single map that showed the path they had taken. This was the first map that had ever been made of the upper Rocky Mountains and the Columbia River from its source to the Pacific Ocean.

> *This was the first map that had ever been made of the upper Rocky Mountains and the Columbia River . . .*

As much as possible, the group ate fresh elk meat. However, the group's original stocks of salt had long run out, and the men craved it to season the meat that they killed. In late December, two members of the party were sent to the ocean to boil salt out of the seawater to use in cooking.

After the meat was butchered, the men smoothed the skins and tanned them to make new clothing. Everyone got a new suit of elk-hide clothes, as well as ten new pairs of moccasins. They would need all they could make.

The Beached Whale

On January 5, 1806, some Indians informed the Corps of Discovery that a whale had washed up on the beach a bit farther south. Sacagawea had come all this way, and she had yet to see the broad, open ocean. She had also never seen a whale before. She begged to be brought along for the trip and Clark obliged her. Clark, Charbonneau, and Sacagawea went to examine the large sea animal. The beached whale stood before them on the sand, but unfortunately, the Clatsop Indians had already stripped most of its meat. Clark then purchased a barrel of whale blubber from them, and they returned to the camp.

Their neighbors, the Clatsop Indians, had previously met and interacted with European sailors who had stopped over in the bay. Many of them spoke a little English. They knew the words for musket and powder and shot. They had also collected a few swear words from visiting sailors and learned how to bargain effectively with the items they sold. Lewis and Clark were dismayed at the prices the Clatsops demanded for fish, whale oil, otter pelts, and other goods that the expedition wanted.

On a few occasions, neighboring Indians stole from the men. They never took anything significant, but the petty theft and the high prices created a guarded atmosphere around Fort Clatsop. Lewis gave the standing order that no Indians were allowed into the fort after dark.

CHAPTER 12

Starting the Return Journey

Altho' we have not fared sumptuously this winter and spring at Fort Clatsop, we have lived quite as comfortably as we had any reason to expect . . .
—Meriwether Lewis, March 20, 1806

By February, Clark's map was done, and it presented a clear picture of their journey to this point. Their travels through the mountains had been crooked, and often aimed in the wrong direction. According to what they had been told, and according to the now completed map, Lewis and Clark could trim almost three hundred miles off the trip. There was a shortcut from Traveler's Rest—as Old Toby had told them—on the western edge of the Rockies, to the Great Falls of the Missouri, on the eastern edge. Instead of following the Missouri River through the mountains, they could cut across land and save weeks of travel.

All the men were more than ready to return home. The constant rain—they only recorded twelve days without it through their whole stay—and the poor food spurred the men to prepare for their journey back. The plan was to leave on the first of April, but everything was ready to go by March 20. New canoes had been built. All the guns were repaired and cleaned. Salt had been made. Each man had new elk-skin clothes and ten new pairs of moccasins. They abandoned Fort Clatsop on March 23, 1806.

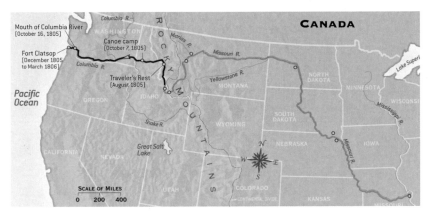

From Traveler's Rest, the Corps of Discovery began its final westward leg, traveling downriver to the Pacific Ocean. They set up Fort Clatsop at the mouth of the Columbia River and spent a difficult winter there from December 1805 to March 1806.

Trouble With the Indians

All of the Indians who lived along the banks of the Columbia River had received the Corps of Discovery with friendship the previous spring. Now, owing partly to familiarity, and perhaps to a change in attitude among the members of the Corps, that sense of friendship was all but gone.

The Indians taunted the men as they paddled and lugged their heavy canoes against the current. "One of them had the insolence to cast stones down the bank at two of the men who happened to be a little detached from the party," Lewis wrote. Even worse, they stole. Crowds of young Indians crept up to the canoes when they were on the shore and picked up what they could grab. Most of the theft was minor—a spoon or a hatchet. On April 11, however, they crossed the line. Three members of a tribe stole Lewis's dog, Seaman.

Lewis sent three of his men to catch the thieves and return his dog. Armed with rifles, the men met no resistance. The

Indians gave up the dog without a fight. Once Seaman was returned to him, Lewis announced that any Indian who even attempted to steal from his men would be put "to instant death."

"Doctor" William Clark

By the time the Corps of Discovery was on its way home, they were completely out of items to trade with the Indians. Still, they would need to buy goods from local tribes. An opportunity presented itself that gave the expedition something to barter with.

On April 28, some injured Indians came to Clark. One had a broken arm, and several had sore eyes. Clark set the broken arm and gave the others a solution to wash their eyes. They soon felt better. Then an Indian man brought his ill wife to Clark. As far as he could tell, she just had a cold, but he gave her all the medicine and care that he could. The Indian man gave Clark a horse as payment. Clark had found a service he could trade.

William Clark continued his "medical practice" as they ascended into the mountains. By the time they reached the Nez Percé tribe, his reputation as a medicine man had preceded him. Indians lined up to be treated for everything from broken bones to sore muscles. While Clark did not have any medical training, he could usually provide some relief for their pain.

Dr. Benjamin Rush gave Lewis a case of medicines, similar to the one in this photograph, for the Corps of Discovery. Clark used the medicines to help local Indians.

Traveling Through Snowy Mountains

In their rush to escape the damp misery of Fort Clatsop, the Corps of Discovery completely outraced the spring. They had reached the Nez Percé village in a little more than a month. Now, even in May, more than ten feet of snow covered all the mountain passes. With the snow completely shrouding the trails, any traveler would probably get lost in the icy wilderness. The Corps had to stop and wait for the snows to clear. Five weeks passed, but the grounds were still covered. Everyone in the Corps wanted to get going again. However, the Indians still told them that a trek into the snow was unwise. Against that advice, the men resolved to restart their journey.

On June 14, the men once again packed up their gear and began the march into the mountains. They tried to find Indians who would accompany them as guides, but none would go so early in the season. Nevertheless, the expedition was going. After three days of traveling, they realized the mess they were in. Snow, as deep as fifteen feet, covered the ground. When Clark reached a peak, he looked out ahead and saw there were no trees to give cover or scraps of bark for the horses to eat. "Under these circumstances," he wrote, "we conceived it madness to . . . proceed without a guide."

This illustration shows the Corps team struggling through the late spring snow that stopped their return trip. They doubled back and waited until they could get Indian guides to show them the way.

Realizing its near mortal error, the Corps of Discovery turned back just far enough to get out of the snow. Meanwhile, they sent Drouillard and Private Shannon back to the Nez Percé village with a spare rifle to act as payment for any Indian who would guide them over the mountains. They returned two days later with three young guides who were the best the tribe had to offer.

One in particular had another reason to help: Clark had mended his broken arm. The Indian was happy to repay the favor. That evening, the Indians performed a ceremony that would bring good weather.

Now, even in May, more than ten feet of snow covered all the mountain passes.

The next day, the expedition was once again on the move. The Indian guides urged the men to travel quickly. Some snow had melted, but there were still long stretches of icy terrain without a trace of food for the horses. In the long days of late June, they traveled eighteen hours a day, from dawn until eleven o'clock at night. No liquid water flowed in the streams, so the men melted snow for themselves and their horses to drink.

A Ceremony for Good Weather

On the evening of June 24, before the expedition started out with the guides, the three Indians gathered some dry tree limbs around some tall trees and "set [them] on fire [creating] a very [sudden] and [immense] blaze from bottom to top of those tall trees." The Indians told Lewis and Clark "that their object in [setting] those trees on fire was to bring fair weather for our journey." The fire rushed up the trunk of the tree. Dead branches near the bottom burst into flames, showering sparks around them. The blazing trees, spraying light and heat all around them reminded Lewis of a fireworks display.

Hot springs like this one gave the men of the Corps their first hot bath in months. The hot spring pictured here is in Yellowstone National Park, where the water is heated by volcanic activity below the earth's surface.

By June 29, they began descending the eastern slope of the mountains. The snow gave way to clear paths and plenty of grass for the horses. That evening the Indians brought the men to some natural hot springs that steamed in the woods. One of the men killed a deer and the group all had a good meal of venison. With their stomachs full for the first time in a few weeks, they also enjoyed their first hot bath in months. The next day they reached Traveler's Rest.

Splitting Up the Expedition

Lewis and Clark decided to divide the Corps of Discovery into two expeditions through the rest of the mountains. Lewis would take ten men and explore the short-cut route across the mountain toward the Great Falls. From there, Lewis planned to take a much smaller group up the Marias River to find its source. The Marias River was the river that the men thought might have been the "true" Missouri as they had traveled west on their way to the Pacific.

Clark and the remaining twenty-one men, plus Charbonneau and Sacagawea, would take a southerly route, retracing part of their journey. When they reached the spot where they had left their canoes the previous year, Sergeant Ordway would take ten men down the Missouri to meet again with Lewis. Clark would explore the Yellowstone River, another great tributary of the Missouri that they had discovered on their journey westward. He would follow this river eastward until he met up with the Missouri—and the rest of the expedition.

Lewis and Clark had previously separated themselves at different points of the journey, but always for just a few days. Now, they planned to be apart for a month. By dividing the large group, they were also dividing the strength of the expedition— and taking a great risk.

On July 3, 1806, Lewis and Clark shook hands and said good-bye to one another. Lewis wrote that he "could not avoid feeling much concern on this occasion." He expected to see his old friend soon enough, but he worried that in the meanwhile something could happen to either one of them. He had no idea how right he was to worry.

Clark's trip down the Yellowstone River was mostly tranquil. This modern photo shows the Yellowstone River winding through Montana's Paradise Valley. It has changed little since Clark discovered it.

CHAPTER 13

Side Trips

The [Blackfeet] Indians rove through this quarter of the country. . . . I wish to avoid an interview with them if possible.
—Meriwether Lewis, July 17, 1806

Lewis's side trip began well. After a dreary winter and a grueling trek up the western lip of the Rockies, the men were grateful to be in game-rich territory. The weather was warm and dry. Once again, the journey took on the atmosphere of a camping trip. The happiness that the men felt was interrupted only by the fear that one of them may be caught off guard by a grizzly bear, or the expedition might encounter Blackfeet Indians—the tribe that the Shoshone feared so deeply. One of the men literally stumbled into a grizzly bear on July 15. He saved himself by smashing the bear in the face with his gun—breaking the weapon and stunning the bear—and then climbing a willow tree. Their worries about the Blackfeet would prove justified as well.

Meeting the Blackfeet

When Lewis's group reached the Marias River, he took three of his men—Drouillard and brothers Reuben and Joseph Field—to explore it. They rode their horses up the banks of the river, and eventually saw that the river veered west. Before turning back, he wanted to note the longitude and latitude. He needed the sun for those readings, but

Lewis took the Field brothers and Drouillard on his side trip to explore the Marias River.

the weather was cloudy. He waited until 9 a.m. the next day before giving up.

The men gathered the horses, and they started down the river, which passed between two hills. Lewis rode his horse to the top of one and scanned the surrounding area. Through his spyglass, Lewis could see seven Indians on horseback. These were Blackfeet. He told the Field brothers to raise the flag. When the Indians saw the flag, they began riding their horses in circles, pointing at it. Lewis's party had only four men, so if the Blackfeet had rifles—and he had every reason to believe they did—Lewis and his men were outnumbered. He decided he would try to make peace.

Lewis and the Field brothers advanced slowly toward the Indians. Now, Lewis counted a total of eight braves. When both groups came within one hundred yards of one another, all the Indians except one stopped. Lewis told the Field brothers to stop. Lewis continued slowly forward. One Blackfoot Indian rode forward from his group and met him. Lewis shook hands with him, and then continued to shake hands with the seven others. The Fields joined the group, and everyone dismounted his horse.

Using sign language, the Blackfeet asked if they had any tobacco. To Lewis, this was a hopeful sign. However, Drouillard, who was off hunting, had the pipe. Lewis sent Reuben Field to get Drouillard. Lewis started interviewing the Blackfeet, who appeared to be teenagers and were as frightened of Lewis as he was of them. He asked who their chief was. The Blackfeet pointed to three braves among them. Lewis thought they looked too young to be chiefs, but he still gave them medals as a gesture of friendship.

Now, Lewis counted a total of eight braves.

Everyone mounted their horses again and rode to meet Reuben Field and Drouillard. They set up a camp together. With Drouillard's help, Lewis spoke with the Blackfeet into the evening. They told Lewis that they were part of a much larger band of Blackfeet who were hunting buffalo a few days away. That night, Lewis took the first watch. He roused Reuben Field at 11:30 to take the next watch. By that time, all the Indians were asleep.

A Killing at Dawn

Joseph Field took the predawn watch. He carelessly laid down his rifle and perhaps dozed a bit. Quietly awakening at dawn, one of the Blackfeet took Joseph's rifle and that of his sleeping brother. Just as the Indian ran off, Reuben woke up and chased him with his knife drawn. He grabbed the Indian, and as they struggled, Reuben drove his knife into the Indian's chest, killing the young brave.

Lewis awoke to the shouts and reached for his rifle. It was gone, so he drew his pistol. He turned and saw an Indian running away with the rifle. Aiming his pistol at the Indian, he shouted at the teenager, who stopped and laid the gun on the ground. Lewis picked up his rifle. As the Indian walked slowly away, the Field brothers requested permission to shoot him. Lewis denied the request.

Meanwhile, another Blackfoot tried to steal Drouillard's rifle. Drouillard wrestled his gun away from the Indian, then requested

Lewis, the Field brothers, and Drouillard awoke to find the Blackfeet trying to steal their guns and horses. A scene from the flight that followed is shown in this painting.

permission to shoot the Indian. Lewis told him no. The Indian was now unarmed.

The men now looked up and saw several of the braves trying to drive off all of their horses. In the chaos of the raid, Indians and horses scattered in all directions. Lewis ran after two Indians with several stolen horses on foot and chased them until they reached a steep bluff where they hid from him in a narrow opening. Lewis shouted that he would shoot if they did not return his horse. One of the Indians jumped out from behind a rock and shouted. Lewis shot him in the belly. The Indian fell to his knees, firing a shot from his own gun. Lewis felt the bullet whiz past his scalp. Without checking to see if the Blackfoot was dead, Lewis returned to camp.

Drouillard wrestled his gun away from the Indian, and then requested permission to shoot the Indian.

The situation was now serious. One young Blackfoot was dead, a second had been shot, and six others had escaped. Lewis knew that when news of the killing reached other Blackfeet, they would send a war party bent on revenge.

Lewis and his men reclaimed, packed, and saddled their horses as quickly as they could and fled. He wanted to meet with the rest of his men as rapidly as possible to strengthen their numbers, but he also worried that the Blackfeet would find the rest of their party and attack before Lewis could warn them. They pushed the horses hard, stopping just long enough to let them eat. When dark came, they killed a buffalo, but carved out only as much meat as they could eat right away. The moon was bright, so they kept running until two in the morning. Finally, they laid down to rest. In one day, they had covered one hundred miles.

Early the next day, Lewis and his men found the rest of their party and told them what had happened. They collected their belongings and continued their flight on the river, abandoning the horses. For the next five days, they kept moving down the Missouri until they were safely beyond Blackfeet territory.

Meeting With Clark

The plan was to meet up again with Clark and half of the Corps of Discovery at the mouth of the Yellowstone River, but when Lewis and his men arrived there, he found a note written by Clark. The mosquitoes in the area were too awful to bear. Clark and his men abandoned the spot and would meet with Lewis several miles farther downriver. Lewis and his men climbed back into their boats and continued on.

The plan was to meet up again with Clark and half of the Corps of Discovery at the mouth of the Yellowstone River.

A few days later, on August 11, they spotted an elk herd north of the river. Lewis and Pierre Cruzatte pulled over to the side of the river to hunt. It was on this occasion that Cruzatte accidentally shot Lewis in his left "thye about an inch below my hip joint." More precisely, he shot Lewis in the butt.

Lewis spent the next few days laying facedown in a pirogue. It hurt too much to sit or lay on his back. On April 12, 1806, Lewis's crew floated into view of Clark's camp. For his part, Clark had had his own adventures in the previous weeks. As planned, he and his group had retraced their steps and traveled back to the Missouri River where the expedition had left the canoes a year ago.

Sergeant Ordway and his men were sent downstream on the Missouri River, while Sacagawea guided Clark, Privates Shields and Shannon, York, Charbonneau, Pompey, and five other soldiers through a mountain pass to the Yellowstone River.

There they built canoes from cottonwood trees, and on July 21, set sail down the Yellowstone River. By August 3, they had reached the Missouri. Barely noticing the explorers floating past them, elk and buffalo crowded the edges of the river. Such abundant game also attracted predators. At night, wolves prowled through the expedition's camp and ate some of the meat the men had left out to dry. On one of the mornings, a grizzly bear tried to swim after the men in their canoes. They shot at the bear as it swam, but only wounded it.

Enormous herds of buffalo crowded the riverside as Clark and his group traveled on the Yellowstone River and onto the Missouri River.

Return to Fort Mandan

Now the Corps of Discovery was together again. They would travel back to the Mandan Village where they had once spent the winter. As they approached the village, they could see that the huts and the stockade they built had been destroyed by an accidental fire. Their friendship with the Mandan, however, remained intact.

Just as they had done almost two years earlier, Lewis and Clark held a formal meeting with the chiefs of the Mandan. This time, they were returning as old friends and, now, trusted allies.

The attempts the Corps had made at forging peace amoung the Indian tribes of the Missouri had failed in their absence. War

This time, they were returning as old friends and, now, trusted allies.

had broken out among several tribes almost as soon as Lewis and Clark sailed from view in April 1805. Lewis and Clark were dismayed over the ongoing warfare. They encouraged the chiefs to travel downriver with them to visit Washington, D.C., but none of the Mandan would go. They feared the Sioux, and they were afraid that they would never return to their home.

After a few days of rest with the Mandan, the preparations for the final leg of the journey began. No longer in need of his services as a translator, Clark paid Toussaint Charbonneau $500 and released him from duty. His departure also meant saying good-bye to Sacagawea and her baby boy Jean Baptiste "Pompey" Charbonneau.

Pompey Charbonneau (1805–1866)

Jean Baptiste "Pompey" Charbonneau traveled from Fort Mandan to the Pacific and back again, before reaching the age of two. He had experienced more adventure before he learned to walk than most people do in an entire lifetime. During this period, Clark had come to be very fond of the baby boy. As he said good-bye to Charbonneau and Sacagawea, he offered to take Pompey with him to St. Louis. Clark promised to raise the boy and pay for his education.

Charbonneau agreed, but told Clark he would have to wait until the boy was old enough to leave his mother. In 1811, Pompey, now about six, went to St. Louis for his education. As he promised, Clark raised him practically as his own, ensuring that he got the education that was promised. The journey that started Pompey's life continued into his adult life. Over the years, he ranged from Europe to California, becoming something of an explorer himself.

Jean Baptiste "Pompey" Charbonneau and his mother Sacagawea were the youngest members of the Corps of Discovery. Pompey went on to be educated in St. Louis.

CHAPTER 14

Home at Last!

Never did a similar event excite more joy throughout the United States.

—Thomas Jefferson

On September 20, 1806, the men of the Corps of Discovery cheered as they caught sight of Holstein cows grazing by the side of the river—a sure sign there was a farm nearby. Three days later, they sailed into St. Louis, firing their rifles as a salute to the town. Residents rushed to the riverbank and let out cheers for the returning explorers.

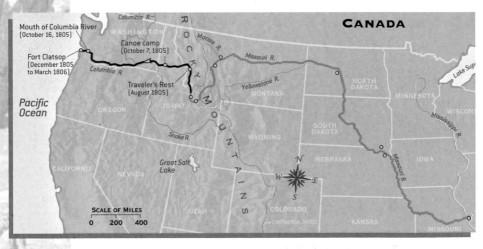

In March 1806, the Corps left Fort Clatsop. At Traveler's Rest, Lewis and Clark split up. Lewis explored a shortcut to the north and had a deadly encounter with the Blackfeet. Clark took a southern route, exploring the Yellowstone River. After the two rejoined on the Missouri River, they returned home, arriving in St. Louis on September 23, 1806.

Jefferson's Reaction to the News

Few Americans can rival Thomas Jefferson in the number and range of his accomplishments. A scholar, a statesman, an architect of modern democracy, even a musician, Jefferson had a lot to be proud of. He was perhaps proudest of Lewis and Clark's accomplishment. Of their journey Jefferson wrote, "Never did a similar event excite more joy throughout the United States. The humblest of its citizens had taken a lively interest in the issue of this journey, and looked forward with impatience for information it would furnish." Jefferson no doubt counted himself among those humble citizens. The explorations of the West had been a lifelong goal of his. Now, as he moved into his second presidential term, he saw that this had been achieved under his presidency.

Lewis and Clark were greeted as heroes when they returned in 1806. This image shows President Jefferson honoring them at the White House.

Lewis, still limping from his gunshot wound, clamored out of his canoe and rushed to the post office. He had to send a letter immediately to the president, informing him of their return. The mail had left for the day, so he sent a messenger by fast horse to the next town, telling the postmaster there to hold the mail until Lewis could finish his letter to President Jefferson.

Peter Choteau, a prominent St. Louis citizen, invited Lewis and Clark as guests of his home. That night, for the first time in nearly two-and-a-half years, the great explorers slept in beds.

Adoration and Praise

The entire city of St. Louis opened itself to Lewis and Clark—the conquering heroes. The people celebrated the duo's return both on the sheer feat of their accomplishment and because it foretold prosperity for the city. The merchants of St. Louis, who had bargained hard with Lewis when he was buying supplies, now anticipated the territory to the west would soon boom with the fur trade. Parties and balls were given in Lewis and Clark's honor.

Lewis, who so desperately missed **cosmopolitan** life during the winter on the Pacific Coast, flourished briefly in the public eye. He traded in his buckskin clothes for a tailored suit and regaled people with tales of their adventures. As he sat smoking cigars

An 1816 etching shows Meriwether Lewis in a full buckskin suit like he would have worn on his return journey from the expedition.

and drinking with the merchants of St. Louis, he reported on the abundant stocks of otter and beaver in the Louisiana Territory. Looking around at his hosts, he saw dollar signs in everyone's eyes—the same that were reflected in his own.

At the beginning of November, Lewis and Clark started for Washington, D.C., to meet with President Jefferson and members of Congress. By the time they arrived at the end of December, Lewis-and-Clark fever gripped the nation. After a seemingly endless series of balls and dinners at every roadside tavern and inn between St. Louis and Washington, the two explorers were treated to yet another formal dinner—this one attended by senators and representatives from all branches of government.

The praise culminated in February 1807 with Jefferson nominating Lewis as the territorial governor of Louisiana. The senate confirmed him in March. Lewis would have dominion over the land he had just explored. His future would never be brighter.

Lewis's Fall from Grace

In March 1808, Lewis returned to St. Louis and took up his duties as governor. Having tried and failed to find a wife, Lewis had become depressed through the previous winter. He struggled to find direction for his life now that the Corps of Discovery was no longer active. He drank too much. However, he looked forward to assuming the job of governor and to seeing William Clark again, who had been appointed the superintendent of Indian affairs in the Louisiana Territory. The two old friends planned to rent a house together. It would be just like old times—except Clark would be bringing his new wife, Julia, with him. Clark had succeeded in romance when Lewis had failed.

Once he moved in with Clark and his wife, Lewis tried his best to stay focused on work—both that of government and of his own investments. However, his judgment, which served him so well in the wilderness, began to fail him.

As the leader of the Corps of Discovery, there was no higher authority than his own. He had also had a blank check from Thomas Jefferson to pay any expenses along the way. Lewis had become accustomed to power, and he had become accustomed to having no real financial responsibility. The job of governor was difficult for Lewis. He needed to build alliances with other government officials but failed miserably.

> *Lewis had become accustomed to power . . .*

In August of 1809, his problems all came crashing down on him. Lewis received a letter from the secretary of war informing him that the government would not pay for certain expenses recently incurred for a military expedition he had sent to Fort Mandan. He was told that he would be personally responsible for the $500 expense—a great deal of money at the time—that was used to purchase additional gifts for the Indians. Lewis had also been borrowing heavily from others to finance land deals, fur trading expeditions, and his growing drinking habit. He was bankrupt, and his reputation was in ruins. His journals were nowhere near being ready to publish, more than two years after the expedition's triumphant return.

Lewis spent three panicked weeks with Clark trying to come up with a plan. The two men agreed that Lewis should go to Washington to defend himself against the claims of misspending.

He left for Washington on September 3, drinking heavily along the way. His mental state deteriorated. He stopped to pick up two army officers, Captain Gilbert Russell and Major James Neely, who would be accompanying him to Washington. On October 10, 1809, they reached an inn outside of Nashville,

Tennessee. Lewis requested a glass of whiskey almost as soon as he climbed down from his horse. His mental and physical state plummeted. After he excused himself from dinner, he went to his bedroom. Through the middle of the night, he paced back and forth. In the predawn hours of October 11, the innkeeper heard a shot. Another soon followed. Meriwether Lewis died at sunrise. Since his death, some people have suggested that Lewis was murdered. However, the two men who knew and cared for him best, William Clark and Thomas Jefferson, always believed that Lewis took his own life.

Clark's Rise to Success

While Lewis tragically could never adjust to life after the return of the Corps of Discovery, Clark thrived. Soon after his marriage to Julia Hancock on January 5, 1808, he assumed his duties as the superintendent of Indian affairs for the Louisiana Territory and excelled in the job.

On January 9, 1809, his wife Julia bore their first child. Clark named the boy Meriwether Lewis Clark, in honor of his old friend Lewis. Clark was able to balance the responsibilities of caring for his family and his complex duties in the territorial government. He was part military man, part diplomat—roles that suited his disposition and tapped into his lifelong experience of dealing with Indians.

A modern rendering of William Clark, shown with maps rolled beneath his arm. Unlike Lewis, Clark became a respected government official after his return from the expedition.

The Scientific Discoveries of Lewis and Clark

President Jefferson gave Lewis and Clark orders not only to travel to the Pacific Ocean and return, but also to make precise records of all the plants and animals they saw on their journey. They succeeded at this, too. Unfortunately, almost no one knew it during the explorers' lifetimes.

Over the course of the trip, they documented 178 plant species and 122 different animal species that were previously unknown to science. These ranged from the grizzly bears they both hunted and feared to the humble prairie dog. Plants, like Lewis's Mock Orange (*Philadelphus lewisii*), and fish, like cutthroat trout (*Oncorhynchus clarki lewisii*), have been given formal Latin names to honor their discoveries. Most of these discoveries were relatively unacknowledged until 1904, when a full, multi-volume, unedited edition of their journals was published by Reuben Thwaites.

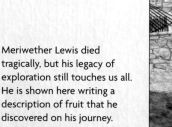

Meriwether Lewis died tragically, but his legacy of exploration still touches us all. He is shown here writing a description of fruit that he discovered on his journey.

In 1813, he took over the job that his old friend had held, that of territorial governor of what was now called the Missouri Territory—the northern portion of the Louisiana Territory. He held the post until 1820 when he lost the election for governor of the newly formed state of Missouri. For the next eighteen years, until his death on September 1, 1838, Clark again focused on Indian matters as the superintendent of Indian affairs at St. Louis. Recognizing his core values of honesty and fairness, the chiefs of the Indian tribes he dealt with treated him as one of their own, calling him The Red Headed Chief.

The Cultural Legacy of Lewis and Clark

The story of Meriwether Lewis and William Clark is a story that defined America—literally and figuratively. The rivers, animals, and mountains they discovered and explored are now synonymous with the American West. The journals they kept—still in print today—provide an adventurer's account that is more true-to-life and at times more poetic than the epic poems of Rome and Greece. History portrays Lewis and Clark as heroes of the developing West. At their core, however, they were simple men with extraordinary drive and courage. With good sense, quick thinking, and sheer guts, they embarked on a dangerous odyssey and returned home in triumph. Their story still resonates today.

Lewis and Clark have been honored on several U.S. postage stamps. This one from 1954 depicts Lewis, Clark, and Sacagewea landing on the shores of the Missouri River.

Glossary

air rifle—type of rifle that shoots a pellet or bullet with the force of compressed air and a spring.

ambushes—surprise attacks on a person or a group of people or troops, usually that are in the process of traveling.

botanist—a scientist who studies plants and plant life.

Continental army—the American army of the Revolutionary War who fought against the British.

corps—A military group consisting of officers and soldiers.

cosmopolitan—sophisticated, with an awareness of global issues.

curing—the process of drying the tobacco leaf so that it is ready for market.

Great Plains—the vast area of land through what is now the Midwest and western portions of the country, characterized by few trees, high grass, and rolling hills.

IOUs—notes that are written as a promise to pay an outstanding debt.

legislature—a body of government charged primarily with writing laws.

midwife—someone who assists a woman giving birth to a child.

minister—a representative or officer of a government.

Native American—any member or descendant of such people who lived in the Americas before the arrival of Europeans. Other terms include American Indian and—as Lewis and Clark would have called various tribes in their time—Indian.

New World—term used by Europeans to describe North and South America and all of the surrounding islands, especially after their discovery and early exploration.

nomadic—a way of life marked by regular periods of travel, usually in a quest for food.

Revolutionary War—the war fought by American colonists against the British that began in 1776; also called the War for Independence.

secretary of state—a high-ranking member of the U.S. president's cabinet, who is charged with overseeing the relationships between the U.S. government and foreign governments.

sextant—a navigational tool used to determine latitude—a grid system used to measure how far north or south one is on the Earth's surface.

surgeon general—the most highly ranked medical doctor in the U.S. government.

the thirteen colonies—thirteen seperate territories founded between 1607 and 1733 ruled by Great Britain.

tracker—a person who can follow the path that a person or animal has taken, usually in the woods or wilderness.

Bibliography

Ambrose, Stephen E. *Undaunted Courage*. New York: Simon & Schuster, 1996.

Allen, John Logan. *Passage Through the Garden; Lewis and Clark and the Image of the American Northwest*. Urbana: University of Illinois Press, 1975.

Bakeless, John Edwin. *Lewis & Clark, Partners in Discovery*. New York: W. Morrow, 1947.

Duncan, Dayton. *Out West: An American Journey*. New York: Viking, 1987.

Foley, William E. *Wilderness Journey: The Life of William Clark*. Columbia: University of Missouri Press, 2004.

Gass, Patrick and Hosmer, James Kendall. *Gass's Journal of the Lewis and Clark Expedition*. Chicago: A.C. McKlurg & Co., 1904.

Holmberg, James J. (ed.) *Dear Brother: Letters of William Clark to Jonathan Clark*. New Haven: Yale University Press, 2002.

Jefferson, Thomas. *The Writings of Thomas Jefferson*. Washington, D.C.: The Thomas Jefferson Memorial Association of the United States, 1907.

Jones, Landon Y. *William Clark and the Shaping of the West*. New York: Hill and Wang, 2004.

Josephy, Alvin M. Jr. and Marc Jaffe. (eds.) *Lewis and Clark Through Indian Eyes*. New York: Knopf, 2006.

Lewis, Meriwether and Clark, William (edited by Thwaites, Reuben). *Original Journals of the Lewis and Clark Expedition, 1804–1806*. New York: Dodd, Mead & Company, 1904–05.

Lewis, Meriwether and Clark, William (edited by Bergon, Frank). *Journals of Lewis and Clark*. New York: Penguin Books, 1989.

Morris, Larry E., *The Fate of the Corps: What Became of the Lewis and Clark Explorers After the Expedition*. New Haven: Yale University Press, 2004.

Source Notes

The following citations list the sources of quoted material in this book. The first and last few words of each quotation are cited and followed by their source. Complete information on referenced sources can be found in the Bibliography.

Abbreviations used:

UC—Undaunted Courage

JLCP—Journals of Lewis and Clark, Penguin edition

WCSW—William Clark and the Shaping of the West

GJLCE—Gass's Journal of the Lewis and Clark Expedition.

WTJ—The Writings of Thomas Jefferson

INTRODUCTION: A Journey Bound by Friendship

PAGE 1 *"Oh [Ocean]…the joy!"*: WCSW, p. 143
PAGE 1 *"Oh [Ocean]…the joy!"*: WCSW, p. 143

CHAPTER 1: Similar Family Backgrounds

PAGE 2 *"No season…his object."*: WTJ, p. 142

CHAPTER 2: Army Life

PAGE 14 *"I am…soldier's life."*: UC, p. 41
PAGE 17 *"I am…soldier's life."*: UC, p. 41
PAGE 17 *"passion…rambling."*: UC, p. 43
PAGE 19 *"Abruptly and…invited there."*: UC, p. 45
PAGE 19 *"fondly hopes…of this nature."*: UC, p. 45

CHAPTER 3: In the Service of Thomas Jefferson

PAGE 21 *"Of courage…[Meriwether Lewis]"*: WTJ, p. 124
PAGE 23 *"This is…than executed"*: UC, p. 69
PAGE 27-28 *"My plan…western ocean."*: UC, p. 98
PAGE 28 *"The enterprise…join you."*: WCSW, p. 113
PAGE 28 *"equal…respects."*: WCSW, p. 113

CHAPTER 4: Preparing for the Expedition

PAGE 29 *"The Object…of commerce."*: WTJ, p. 148

CHAPTER 5: Getting Under Way

PAGE 38 *"Set out…on the bank."*: JLCP, p. 4
PAGE 40 *"…a fair evening…himself at 20 feet."*: JLCP, p. 4

CHAPTER 6: The Sioux Nation

PAGE 48 *"The [Sioux]…well made."*: JLCP, p. 40
PAGE 50 *"with paint, …of different colors."*: JLCP, p. 40
PAGE 51 *"all things…of necessity."*: JLCP, p. 51
PAGE 51 *"We are friends…any Indians."*: JLCP, p.51
PAGE 52 *"my soldiers…a single day."*: GJLCE, p. 37.

CHAPTER 7: Fort Mandan

CHAPTER 8: Finding the Great Falls

CHAPTER 9: The Shoshone Tribe

CHAPTER 10: Journey Down the Rapids

CHAPTER 11: Fort Clatsop

CHAPTER 12: Starting the Return Journey

CHAPER 13: Side Trips

CHAPTER 14: Home at Last!

Image Credits

About the Author

John Burrows is the pen name of John McCloskey who has published a version of the Robin Hood stories in *The Adventures of Robin Hood*. He also writes articles on subjects ranging from electronic books to rodent control. John lives in New York City.